Sins from the Past

By

J. Aundre Clinton

This book is a work of fiction. Places, events, and
situations in this story are purely fictional. Any
resemblance to actual persons, living or dead, is
coincidental.

ISBN: 1-4033-6492-3 (e-book)
ISBN: 1-4033-6493-1 (Paperback)

This book is printed on acid free paper.

1stBooks - rev. 10/23/02

THE AUTHOR THANKS...

On this day, I'm extremely grateful and to many I am very thankful. First, I would like to give glory to God for his many blessings and for giving me the gift of writing. Through God all things are possible and without Faith there is nothing!

To my mother, Estella M. Clinton, you have truly been an inspiration. Thank you for all the love and support you have given me over the years and for instilling in me the belief that if I put my mind to something I can achieve anything. Love you!

To my brother and sisters- Peter, Leslie, Alexis and Rosland- thank you for your support and love. You mean the world to me!

To my nieces and nephews- D'Andra, Shakira, D'Mya, Wa'Vay and DeMarcus- Accept only the best that life has to offer! I love you.

To one of the most remarkable guys on the planet, Kenneth McCants. I am indeed blessed to be your friend. You are so dear to me and your friendship has been invaluable. Thank you for believing in me! I couldn't have done this without you. My love to you! Oh, I'm still mad you went to Paris without me. Smile.

Brian Spurlock...You are truly a beautiful young man. Your friendship over the years has meant a lot to me. Thank you for your love and support! Thank you for keeping it real and encouraging me when I wanted to give up! You are truly a "Diamond in the Rough!"

To Dane Cornelius...What can I say? You and I have been friends for over ten years now, and you have become like a brother to me. You are one of the most loving people that I know. Thank you for believing in me! I am truly honored and blessed to have a friend like you. I wish you joy and happiness in your life!

Omenicia "Nici" Davis. What's up Miss Country Grand? (LOL)...I want to thank you for your support and friendship. You were one of the bright spots at work. I could always count on you putting a smile on my face with your stories. One more thing, buy your own Little Debbie's and stop eating mine (smile). Hugs and Kisses.

Haddy Lowe...You provided me with support and encouragement from the beginning. I thank you from the bottom of my heart. You are a beautiful young lady, and I'm going to be on the front row when you're working that runway. Forget me not!

Jerence "Jaboo" Haugabook. The finest country boy I know (smile). You have brought unspeakable joy into my life from the day we first met over two years ago. You are still just as crazy then as you are now. Thank you for always putting a smile on my face! Love you like crazy!

Isaac Snipe III...You're one in a million. Thank you for standing beside me! Sweet kisses.

Anthony Watson, my tennis buddy. You put a smile on my face every time I hear you scream your name when you miss a shot. "Tony...you stupid little black boy." I knew one day I would meet someone as crazy as me. You are a beautiful person, and it has been my pleasure knowing you. Thanks for keeping it real!

To the tennis crew- Darryl P., Brian M., Clay K., Anthony G., V. Scott. It truly has been a pleasure knowing you guys. You have made tennis very fun and enjoyable. Thank you! Let's get on the court soon!

Brandy Piggie (Sisitergirl)...I miss you so much. Your beautiful personality made my day. You are truly a joy to be around, and I'm glad to call you my friend. Hurry up and get your butt back to the Atl. Holla!

N.K.B.- my friend who wants to be referred to as the "Governor". I want to thank you for believing in me. You are a handsome, intelligent young man. Your humble nature warms my heart every time I'm in your presence. Success is yours!

Derrick Wheeler…I'm so glad that I met you. Your warm smile is infectious. Thank your for your support and encouragement. Now finish that book that you've been working on! I got my checkbook ready to buy it.

Delvon Cunningham…Thank you for first believing in me! When your book is published, I'm gonna be the first one in line to buy it. Keep smiling my handsome prince!

To Jerry Huff…It has been a pleasure knowing you all these years. I still can't believe you didn't like my meatloaf (smile). I still love you anyway. Stay sweet my friend. Always remember, I'm the cute one. LOL

To Earl Thomas, Ed.D…I want to thank you for you support and guidance over the years. You have always believed in me and always said that I was gifted. The moment of truth has arrived and now you can see the fruit of our deep discussions. I tip my hat to you. You're simply the best!

To Travis Hunter, Bestselling Author…It was truly a pleasure to meet you. Thank you for sharing your knowledge with me! It has been extremely helpful. You are a gifted writer, and I have enjoyed reading your work. I wish you continued success!

To Gary Wilson…Thank you for your encouraging words! You are truly a beautiful young man. Stay sweet and go after your dream! I'm going to be on the front row giving my support when you on that runway. Smooches!

To the many others who have made this more than just a possibility, thank you!

Finally, this author would like to thank you, the reader, for your support.

Until next time…J. Aundre' Clinton…Atlanta, Georgia.

Dedicated in Loving Memory

FOR MY GRANDMOTHER, ALICE B. HANDY
(1904 – 1988)
FOR TEACHING ME UNCONDITIONAL LOVE
AND FOR TEACHING ME HOW TO PRAY

I MISS YOU SO MUCH! ALL MY LOVE TO
YOU!

In Memory

Jessie P. Clinton, Mary L. Handy-Dunlap, Mary
Jones, Grover "Bill" Handy

Tracy Tibbs, Rodney Coleman, Essex Hemphill,
LeWan Alexander

CHAPTER ONE

Sincerely, Mr. Greene

Who said that life was going to be fair?

I had pondered this question over a thousand times in my mind. I could never come up with a good answer. It appeared to me that bad people always enjoyed life, and the good people always suffered. Big Mama would say, "Dae'Mon, that's me, good people will get their reward in the end when they reach the gates of heaven."

I wasn't so sure about that because the state my personal life was in made it appear that I had reached the gates of hell. I had made two bad relationship choices in the past that left me feeling empty on the inside and yearning for more. I vowed to never love again and was successful for five years. Then, I met someone who offered promises of love, hope and prosperity. I fell deeply in love. Unlike the others though, my heart was left with a wound that was so severe that I wasn't sure if I would recover.

And I was left questioning myself, how did this happen to me?

CHAPTER TWO

NEW YEAR'S EVE 1998

A new blanket of snow had just fallen on the city, which caused the wind chill factor to dip to minus five. The sky was dark gray with no hints of clouds in sight. The scene was reminiscent like that out of a horror movie. Yet it was peaceful and serene.

My mind became filled with thoughts of how to bring in the New Year. I wanted to attend the New Year's Party at Connections, but I wasn't about to brave the cold air or the slippery roads. Kansas City could get bitterly cold in the winter. So, I decided to find something in the kitchen to drink. I had liquor left over from a party my best friend, Kevyn, hosted at my loft three months earlier.

I looked in the cupboards and found a bottle of Gin. I decided to have Gin and Juice, since orange juice was the only beverage I had in the refrigerator other than Kool-Aid. Gin and Kool-Aid! I don't think so!

I had a serious case of the holiday blues. It was obvious because I usually didn't drink under any circumstances. I always felt that the holidays were just a means of making single people realize just how alone they were. Could it be a Conspiracy?

I was in a funk, and it didn't help that I was watching "Waiting To Exhale" for the third time that day. I became prisoner to thoughts of my first relationship when I was in high school. My first love!

His name was Edwin Harris who I met when I started my sophomore year at County High School in Pecan Grove, a small town in Mississippi. We were in the same homeroom class, and I was mesmerized from the moment I first set eyes on him as he came strolling into the classroom. He was so beautiful! He had a slender defined build, dark skinned and bow-legged with a face that I personally would have put on Mount Rushmore. I wanted him so bad that I could taste it.

I fantasized about Edwin for weeks. I envisioned all the things that I would do to him which resulted in a lot of wet dreams. I got so aroused one night that I had to get up to take a cold shower at 3 in the morning. Scandalous! I never imagined that I would get a chance to live out my fantasy.

It came to pass when Edwin approached me one beautiful fall afternoon as I was headed to my fifth period class. I almost died when he said my name, "Dae'Mon". It sounded so sweet rolling off his tongue. If I were a bomb, I would have exploded on the spot. I turned slowly gazing into his beautiful brown eyes. He wanted tutoring to prepare for our upcoming midterm exam.

"A brotha needs help with this algebra. Man, can you help me out? I'll properly compensate you." Edwin said.

I wasn't about to let my dream man slip through my fingers, so I jumped for the opportunity. "Yeah, I'll help you out. Just let me know what I can do for you!" I said in a seductive voice.

We agreed to hook up...I mean get together to study the following evening at my place. We exchanged numbers as we casually strolled down the hall. Of course, I was in heaven! I walked into my classroom in a daze, and it wasn't until I walked into the trashcan that I snapped back to reality.

Edwin arrived at my house in a tank top and form fitting nylon shorts. It took all my power to keep from jumping his bones the moment he walked through the door. I gathered myself and escorted Edwin to my bedroom, located in the back of the house, to begin studying. We took a seat at my makeshift desk that I constructed out of a large wooden table my daddy was about to throw out. I was seated in one of the chairs from the kitchen table, and Edwin was seated in Big Mama's old rocking chair that she had given me a few years back.

We were not fifteen minutes into the study session before Edwin began to blow in my ear. I was nervous and became afraid as to what was going to happen next. I was a virgin, so this was all new to me. I had never kissed anyone before let alone had sex, especially with a man. The porno movie I had watched didn't prepare me for this.

I turned slightly to my right to avoid his mouth all the while not looking up from my algebra book. I tried to stay focused on the page until he grabbed me and kissed me on the lips. It was a long passionate kiss that set off fireworks. Stars and Stripes Forever! I enjoyed the feel of his tender lips pressed against mine. I didn't want to come off as being soft, so I jumped up and shouted obscenities.

"Man, what the fuck are you doing?"

"Just relax." Edwin said as he grabbed my arm.

He pulled me onto his lap. He began to kiss me again, but this time he forced my lips apart. I was in ecstasy as he tickled the back of my throat with his tongue.

I began to resist but to no avail. Edwin pushed me to the floor and climbed on top of me. He assured me that all he wanted was to have a little fun. I don't have to get into what fun he wanted. All I can say is we continued to have fun for the next three years.

During the course of our affair, Edwin would vow his love to me. He often said that once we graduated we would move away together, so we would no longer have to deny our love for each other. I, of course, believed every word. Well, my joy didn't last for long. On the first day of class of our senior year, I found out that Edwin impregnated one of my classmates. I was devastated to say the least.

Edwin vowed that the baby would not interfere with our relationship. He said that his mother would take care of the child once he left for college, and we could assume the parenting role together once we graduated. I wanted to leave him alone at that point but I couldn't. I was too weak to just walk away. The thought of Edwin's proposal made me happy and sad at the same time. I was sad because I would have to share his love, and I was happy because I could still be with him. In the end, I forgave him for his transgression and assumed my duties as his devoted lover.

Once again, my joy was short lived. Graduation day rolled around, and I was excited about graduating from high school and moving to Kansas with Edwin. I was equally joyous when Edwin called stating he wanted to see me later that evening and to meet him at our usual hideout in the country on Section Five. I thought it was going to be a night to remember, and it was.

"Dae'Mon, I can't see you anymore. It's time for me to be a man and take care of my child."

I was in shock and couldn't believe what I was hearing. I understood what he was saying, but I thought about the promises that he made to me.

"What about us moving to Kansas together?"

"What the fuck did I say? I don't want to see yo punk ass anymore!" He screamed at the top of his lungs.

I began to cry, which Edwin found to be very irritating.

"Stop acting like a bitch and be a man!" He shouted.

I headed to my car, but before I could open the door, Edwin grabbed me by the arm and looked into my eyes. If looks could kill! He pointed his finger at me and said, "If you tell anyone about us, I promise I will fuck you up!"

My tears turned into a loud sob as I got in the car to drive away.

Edwin began shouting, "Faggot! You fucking faggot! Get your faggot ass out of my face!" I drove home and told no one of what had transpired over the past three years.

The rest of the summer was a blur after that night. I cried on a daily basis as I thought of Edwin. My heart had been broken, and I was in deep pain. I didn't understand how he could just up and throw me away after all that time of loving me. I gave him my heart, and he stepped on it like a cheap rug.

I left for college later that summer and vowed that I would never venture down the avenue of love again for I had learned my lesson.

Even though it had been almost ten years since that incident, it still made me angry just to think about how I was treated. Bastard!

I snapped back to reality and continued to ponder what I was going to do to celebrate the New Year.

CHAPTER THREE

I had been sitting reminiscing about the past so long that the New Year had slipped up on me. It was officially 1999!

I decided to make a toast and go to bed. I was hoping to get a buzz that would make me sleep soundly. "Here's to a New Year with promises of happier times ahead. Here's to a year where all of my wishes will come true. Here's to a year that I will become more sociable and not be afraid to love and be loved." Yeah right! I needed to get serious I thought to myself. I made the same toast every year, and before the end of January, I was back in the same old rut. It was a nice thought anyway!

"Through the teeth, through the gums, look out belly, here it comes!" I said aloud. Whew! The drink was nasty. I didn't realize I had made it so strong. My mouth felt as if it was on fire. "That's it, no more drinking for me!" I vowed.

I got in bed only for the phone to start ringing. I picked up after the second ring.

"Who dis?" I inquired.

"The man of your dreams." said the deep voice.

"Really? How do I know you?"

"We met last week," the voice responded.

"Yeah right, where?" I said trying to distinguish the voice.

"The grocery store in the produce section."

"Produce Section? Kevyn, I'm gonna kick your ass!"

"Got you, didn't I?" Kevyn laughed.

"I knew it was you. You hateful piece of trash."

We laughed.

"Happy New Year!" Kevyn said.

"The same to you. What's up, boy?" I said as I sat up in the bed.

"Bored as hell!"

"I know what's coming next!"

"What are you talking about?" Kevyn said.

"You're gonna try to drag me out to the club with you right?"

"Not exactly!"

"What? Are you ill?" I laughed.

"Very funny, witch! No, I want to go to the New Year's Bash on 12th and Hardesty."

"Umm huh!"

"Listen before you say no!"

"Ok, I'm listening," I said.

"They have a DJ there from DC, strippers, food and all you can drink. What do you say?"

"Strippers! I say I'll be ready in 20 minutes."

"You won't regret this. I promise."

"I know I won't. Did you call Justice?" I questioned.

"No, I don't feel like Ms. Justice this evening." Kevyn said in an exasperated tone.

"Why is that?"

"Cuz every time we go out, she is always trying to cock block. He's not cute enough, Kevyn. He's a gold digger. He's a tramp…It's like whatever! I don't feel like her shit tonight. I want to go out and have a good time." Kevyn snapped.

"Ok, my brother. I was just asking. You don't have to bite my head off." I said defensively.

"I'm sorry but she can really work my nerves at times. I want some holiday loving, and I don't need Mother Justice getting in my way. You know she would fuck up a wet dream!"

We laughed.

"You still have those?" I said after catching my breath.

"No darling, I get too much action to need a wet dream. The only thing that's wet is the sheets afterwards."

"You nasty boy. I didn't know you had in ya." I said.

"You'll find out one of these days." Kevyn stated.

"I would much rather mud wrestle a pig."

"Whatever floats your boat!" Kevyn responded.

We laughed.

"Anyone ever tell you that you're crazy as a road lizard?"

"Every day and twice on Sunday. Charter even turned me down." Kevyn joked.

"Let me get off this phone so I can wash my stuff."

"Why? It's not like you're going to let anyone play with it." Kevyn said.

"You damn right! They haven't proven themselves worthy. Besides, I'm not like a birthday cake where everybody gets a piece."

"Yeah, but I'm gonna get some of your stuff sooner than later! Kevyn said as he quickly hung up the phone.

5…4…3…2…1…Just as I expected! I knew he would call back.

"House of Beauty this is cutie." I said.

"May be the House of Beauty, but you ain't no cutie." Justice said laughing.

"Oh I see you're wearing that new fragrance?" I countered.

"What new fragrance?" Justice asked.

"Jealousy."

We laughed.

"Good one! Happy New Year, baby boy! What's happening?" Justice said.

"The same to you. Getting ready to hit the streets."

"Where are you and Kevyn going?" she asked.

I tried to think of a quick lie. "Nowhere, I'm getting ready for bed." I said.

"Yeah right, Dae'Mon! He doesn't want me to go with you guys, does he?" Justice questioned.

"Go where?" I replied.

"Dae'Mon, don't lie!" Justice snapped.

"I'm telling you the truth. I'm getting ready for bed and I haven't spoken to Kevyn," I lied again.

"Ok, I know you're lying, but I'll let you slide this time. Anyway, I'm getting ready to head over to this party at 12th and Hardesty. Would you care to join me?" Justice asked.

"12th and Hardesty? Isn't that where Pat's joint is?" I asked.

"Yes."

"You're going there by yourself?"

"Dae'Mon, you know that you and Kevyn are going to be there. I don't know why you keep lying about it." Justice snapped.

"Look, I told you I'm not going anywhere. If you don't believe me, why don't you call Kevyn for yourself and ask him." I countered.

"I'll do just that! Then, I'm cussing both of you out." She said.

"Just call him before I come over there and kick yo ass!"

"Hold on!" Justice said as she clicked over to the other line to call Kevyn.

I knew things were about to get ugly. Justice knew I was lying and Kevyn would have been mad at me if I told Justice we were going. Oh well, they both would just have to get over it.

"You there?" Justice said as I heard the ringing of a phone.

"Yes, I'm here." I said.

"I'm going to read both of you bitches." Justice said as Kevyn answered the phone.

"Hello." Kevyn said.

"Bitch, why didn't you tell me you guys were going to Pat's party!" Justice said to Kevyn.

"You wait one damn minute, Miss Thing! Don't you ever call my mothafucking house talking like that again." Kevyn said in a nasty tone.

"Hey Kevyn." I said trying to intervene.

"Bitch, I'll come over there and beat your ass! Justice said.

"Bring it on bitch!" Kevyn responded.

"Alright, that's enough! Both of you stop it, right now!" I screamed into the phone.

"No, I'm tired of her always trying to read me and get on my case." Kevyn said.

"I just asked you a simple question. You're the one acting an ass." Justice said.

"Ok, I'll say this one last time! Knock it off! Now, the reason for this call is because Justice called me to say that she is going to Pat's party and wanted to know if we were going. I explained to her that we were not going, but she thinks I'm lying. So, Kevyn, will you please explain to Justice that we didn't have any plans to go there?" I said trying to keep the lie concealed.

"I don't have to explain anything to that bitch. If she wants to go, let her go." Kevyn said as he slammed the phone down.

"Ooh, that stupid mothafucker makes me sick!" Justice screamed.

"Justice, that is no way to talk about one of your best friends." I said.

"Whatever Dae'Mon! I thought you were better than that. I cannot believe you would lie to me just to protect Kevyn. We all are supposed to be friends. Some friends you guys are! Instead of watching my enemies, I need to watch you and Kevyn. You bitches are trifling!" Justice said as she disconnected the line.

I got read. Oh no, I was not about to take that lying down. I quickly got dressed, so I could let them have it.

11

CHAPTER FOUR

A warm peaceful evening had turned into a disaster. Tempers were hot as a major catfight had just occurred. The claws were protruding ready to do damage. Just to think it all started because I was too afraid to tell the truth. Stupid!

I loved Kevyn and Justice dearly, but they both could really work my nerves. Neither one wanted to step back or give in! They would fight until the finish. For what? Foolish Pride!

Kevyn could only take Justice in doses. And Justice loved to ruffle Kevyn's feathers just to keep things stirred up. It was a love/hate relationship. I never understood that about them. They had been friends for a long time. In fact, I met Kevyn through Justice.

It was an unusually stressful Friday at work. I needed to unwind, so I decided to try my luck in Westport, the midtown area of Kansas City. The place where all the cool people went to party. Not that I considered myself cool, but I could hold my own. Thank you ever so much!

I found myself at the Coliseum. A local bar that was known for its' gay clientele on Thursday nights. Since it was Friday, I didn't think I would be approached by anyone. All I wanted was a Ginger Ale and to be left alone. However, I was approached by a beautiful woman who took a seat next to me at the bar. She was a creature of regal beauty. She stood about 5'8" and weighed in at about 120 pounds with cinnamon brown skin and a shape to die for a la Vanessa L. Williams.

"Hello, my name is Justice. You are?"

I couldn't help but to notice that she was dressed in a beautiful pinned stripe dress suit. I didn't know much about women clothing, but that outfit looked expensive like a Donna Karen original.

"I'm Dae'Mon." I replied.

12

"It's a pleasure Dae'Mon." Justice said as she extended her hand.

Being the perfect gentleman, I kissed the back of her hand. I could tell she enjoyed the kiss. She flirted with me for half an hour before she realized that I wasn't responding. She got the hint and finally asked, "Are you gay?"

I quickly responded, "Yes."

Not even a woman as beautiful as Justice could make me forget the fact that I was attracted to men! Under ordinary circumstances (heterosexual man), I could see myself with a woman like her. She epitomized class and carried herself like a star, which explained her "I Am All That" attitude. That was why she and Kevyn didn't always get along cuz he thought he was all that too.

Judging by the look on her face, she was shocked that I was so opened and honest with her about my sexuality. Hey, as long as Big Mama loved me for who I was I didn't give a damn what anyone else thought!

"What a waste!" Justice whispered under her breath.

"What do you mean? How is that a waste?" I retorted.

"You're a fine man and any woman would love to get her hands on you."

"Yeah, I 'm sure they would just as any man would love to get his hands on me too. Sweetheart, I don't mean to be rude, but I would like to be alone."

"Oh, are you having a bad day?" Justice said in a sympathetic voice. "Tell mother all about it."

"I rather not."

"Hey, can I ask you something?"

"Oh God! What now?" I sighed.

"Don't be so hateful! Loosen up."

"Alright! What now?"

Justice rolled her eyes and said, "Do you have a man?"

"My aren't we getting personal?"

"No, the reason I asked is because I have a friend that I think you would be a perfect match for."

I laughed.

"Is that so! Well, I hate to burst your bubble, but I'm not looking for a man or anything else right now.

I was still getting over my last relationship and wasn't entertaining the thoughts of dating anyone. Yes, I was still bitter.

"Why are you being such a bitch?" Justice said with a smile on her face.

"The same reason why you're being a smartass." I said with an even bigger smile.

"I'm just trying to be friendly. Since I can't have you I would love to be your friend and hook you up with my homeboy."

"No thanks! I have had my fair share of hookups, so if you would excuse me." I said as I rose to my feet.

"Wait, here comes my friend now." Justice said as she put her hand on my arm.

I noticed a very attractive man approaching us from the backside of the bar. How do I describe him? Well, he was sporting what appeared to be an Armani suit, form fitting body shirt that hugged his chiseled chest. He had a baldhead with a neatly trimmed goatee, beautiful brown eyes to compliment his paper-sack brown skin. This guy really had it going on. I was in awe, so I quickly took my seat. Shut up! You would have done the same thing!

Justice quickly rose to her feet to greet her friend. They gave each a smirk on the lips and a big hug. It wasn't a passionate kiss, but more of a kiss between friends. I could tell they were very close. Suddenly, the friend noticed me and was more than eager to explore further.

"Justice, who is your friend?" the guy asked.

"Kevyn, I would like to introduce you to Dae'Mon."

"Hello, Mr. Dae'Mon." Kevyn said as he extended his hand.

We shook hands while giving each other the once over. I was impressed with him, as he was equally impressed with me. My 6'1", 160-pound build was something to behold. Going to the gym had its' advantages!

"Hello, it's a pleasure to meet you, Kevyn." I said as I removed my hand from his grip.

"Dae'Mon, this is the friend that I was telling you that I wanted you to meet." Justice said with a cheesy grin on her face.

It was almost as if they had ESP or something. Kevyn turned on his charm and started trying to work me like yesterday's pork chop. As flattered as I was, I was not about to let him think that I was easy. So I put on my tough guy role.

"So, Dae'Mon, what brings you in here on a Friday night alone?" Kevyn said.

"I just needed to unwind from the days' events. That's all."

"Really now! So where's your girl?"

I was about to go off on him for asking a stupid question, but he was cute. So, I decided to play along.

"I don't have a girlfriend, Kevyn. Justice didn't tell you that I like men?" I said while trying to contain my laughter.

"I would have never guessed. Well I do too."

"Ok, I can see where this is going. I will check you guys later." Justice said as she disappeared out of sight. I suddenly became nervous. I was left alone with a fine man. Mercy!

"You two had this planned from the beginning?" I questioned.

"I don't know what you're talking about, Dae'Mon! What makes you think we're up to something?" Kevyn said with a sly grin on his face.

"I wasn't born yesterday, Kevyn. I know Justice was trying to set us up!" I countered.

"She's always looking out for my best interest."

We sat at the bar and talked for what appeared to be hours. I found Kevyn to be a very deep brotha, but relationship material he was not. I could tell just by the way he was carrying on about different things such as money, his appearance, etc. He just seemed to be so self-absorbed yet so secure with himself. He came across as a man who loved himself and expected everyone else to love him just as much.

I enjoyed the fact that he was a great conversationalist and not afraid to go after what he wanted. He admitted that he was attracted to me and would like to get to know me better. Against my better judgment, I went out on a date with him. The maintenance cost was too expensive. It has always been said that two high maintenance people should not get together. Kevyn and I were no exception. As a result, our love affair never quite got off the ground. Kevyn always referred to me as the one who got away. Meaning that he never got a chance to taste my juices! If you catch my drift?

Over the next several months, I spent a lot of time with Kevyn and Justice. We had become a small family. You couldn't find one without finding the other two somewhere near. They called themselves teaching me the ropes on how to land a good man. Mind you, they were both single. I enjoyed their tricks, but I wasn't having it. I wasn't ready to venture down "Pain Ave." again.

They had been very supportive of me. I knew I couldn't have made it the past three years without them. When I was with them, I could forget my troubles until they would try to set me up with someone. I guess I had always been afraid that if I allowed someone new in my life, then my extended family would disappear. They were both too important to me to allow that to happen.

That was why I couldn't allow my best friends to be at odds. I had to calm the storm. They were both stubborn and pig headed to admit when they were wrong. So, I had to be the diplomatic one to restore the peace. That was not going to be an easy task. They both were angry and said hurtful things to one another, so it was going to take a lot of convincing to get them to talk again. Oh boy!

CHAPTER FIVE

I was headed south bound on Troost Ave. when I hit a patch of ice. My car slid into the curve, and my heart almost stopped. I caught my breath thinking of how foolish it was to drive on the icy roads just to get Kevyn and Justice to reconcile. I should have taken my ass to bed. However, I was already out, so I decided to try my luck with Kevyn since he lived about five blocks from me. I turned onto 10th street and headed over to Wabash. I was hoping he was not still fuming cuz if he were I wouldn't hear the end of it.

I parked my car on the side of the curve and almost slipped trying to get out. I made it to Kevyn's apartment and knocked on the door!

"Who is it?" Kevyn said behind the closed door.

"It's Dae'Mon."

Kevyn slowly opened the door. "Come in. What are you doing here, Dae'Mon?"

"Hey baby," I said ignoring his question. I gave him a hug as he closed the door behind me. "It's cold out there."

"What do I owe the pleasure of this visit?" Kevyn said with a quizzical look on his face.

"Can't I come to visit my best friend?" I said as I wiped my feet on the welcome mat.

"Yes, but this late and in this weather! You know how you always carry on about the weather and the roads. So what gives Dae'Mon Latrell Greene?

Kevyn was obviously curious to know the reason for my visit since he didn't normally use my full name unless he was annoyed with me.

"I came to say I love you."

"Dae'Mon, don't play! Tell me the truth before I put you back out in the cold!

"Ok, I came to get you and Justice to make up."

"Please, don't tell me that bitch is outside!" Kevyn said as he rolled his eyes.

"No, I was hoping that we could drive over to her place and then to the party!" I said with a cheesy smile on my face as I stood near the door.

"Dae'Mon, you know I love you, don't you? But it'll be a cold day in hell before I make up with that self-righteous bitch!" Kevyn said as he plopped down on his leather black sofa.

"Please!" I begged. "I'll wash your feet."

Kevyn laughed. "Darling, don't beg! It's not becoming of you."

"I'll give you a kiss!"

"Thanks! As much as I would love to, but I'm afraid I'll have to pass."

"There is nothing I can do to convince you to clear the air with Justice?" I questioned as I took a seat next to Kevyn.

"I'm afraid not, so if you wouldn't mind please drop it!"

"Ok, so can we at least go to the party?"

"Yes, I would love to accompany you." Kevyn said as he jumped up from the sofa. "I'll be ready in 10 minutes."

Kevyn disappeared into the bathroom to get dressed. I had a plan. Since I couldn't get them to communicate. I would just have both of them show up at the party. This way they would be forced to talk or kill each other. Dilemma! Dilemma! I decided to do it. I grabbed the phone located on the end table next to the sofa to call Justice.

"Hello, Justice speaking."

"Hey, baby!" I said.

"Dae'Mon, where are you?"

"At home." I lied. Thank God she didn't have caller ID!

"No, you're not! I just called you a few minutes ago to apologize"

"Yes, I'm home. I was in the bathroom. Anyway, I was calling to have you meet me at 12th and Hardesty."

"Why? I can't believe you're willing to drive in this weather!" Justice said.

"Well I'm feeling it this evening and besides you said you wanted to go. Have you changed your mind?"

"No, I haven't. Is Kevyn coming with you?"

"Why do you ask?"

"Cuz if he is, I'm not!"

"You shouldn't be like that. He is one of your best friends or have you forgotten?" I said.

"Yeah, yeah whatever! You never answered my question!"

"What question?" I said playing dumb.

"Don't play with me Dae'Mon! You know damn well what I asked you. Is Kevyn going to be there?"

"For the last time, NO!" I lied. I was gonna have to say a thousand Hail Mary's to be forgiven for all the lies I had told in one night.

"What time are you going to be there?"

"In about 20 minutes. It's 12:45 now, so I should be there by 1:15."

"Ok, I'll see you there! Oh, Dae'Mon if you're lying about Kevyn being there, it's your ass." Justice said as she hung up the phone.

Well I guess it was going to be my ass then!

I didn't feel that it was wrong of me to get my best friends back on speaking terms. They were too dear to me to allow this to continue another minute. I had to admit that I was somewhat nervous. I was hoping my little scheme didn't blow up in my face. If I couldn't get them to squash this problem, it would be World War III at the party, for they would both come after me for my deception. Help me!

"Dae'Mon, who are you talking to?" Kevyn screamed from the bathroom.

"No one." I lied. "I was singing."

"Ok, my bad. I thought you were on the phone."

"Yeah, talking to my baby's daddy!" I laughed.

20

"That would be a miracle since you don't give it up." Kevyn said while entering the living room.

"You can go straight to hell. You just mad cuz you can't get it."

"Listen, I could have had that raggedy stuff of yours if I really wanted it." Kevyn laughed. "I was just being a gentleman."

"Now that's funny! When have you ever not wanted a piece of ass?" I questioned.

We laughed.

"Let's go before I take some now."

"Over my dead body."

"Well, if that's the way you like it, who am I to judge?" Kevyn said with a comical look on his face.

"Let's go, tramp. You wouldn't know what to do with me anyway."

"Remember, you're on my turf. So, don't make me show you!"

"Enough said, let's go." I said as we headed out the door.

Kevyn closed the door behind us and activated the intrusion alarm. We walked hand and hand to his car in silence. Suddenly, Kevyn broke the silence.

"Are you leaving your car here, Dae'Mon?"

"No, why don't you follow me back to my place, so I can leave it there."

"Ok."

I drove my car to my loft and parked it in front of the building. I was thinking to myself that I should drive to the party just in case Kevyn and Justice put on a show when they saw each other. I had a feeling that everything would work out for the best. They had too much history to allow just one fight to end their friendship. It wasn't like they hadn't fought before.

"Dae'Mon, may I ask you something?" Kevyn said as I climbed into his car.

"Yes."

"Do you ever wonder what could have become of us?"

"Kevyn are you getting sentimental on me?" I laughed.

"I'm serious. Do you think we could have had a successful relationship?"

"Kevyn, I love you dearly. But to be honest, I don't think we could have. Let's face it...You think very highly of yourself, very highly; and if you meet someone who doesn't think as highly of you, there's bound to be problems. The problem is that we both think very highly of ourselves and that spelled disaster from day one."

"Yeah, I know!" Kevyn said with a sad look on his face.

"Kevyn, what made you ask that question? I mean we went out on one date three years ago."

"It's a New Year and I guess I'm feeling sentimental like you said. Would you go out with me again?"

"What?" I said with a puzzled look on my face. "Kevyn, where is all of this coming from? I've never seen you like this in the three years I've known you. Have you been drinking?"

"No, I haven't been drinking. It's just that I've just gotten to a point in my life where I'm ready to settle down. I can't think of anyone better than you that I would rather be with."

"Oh my God, have you completely lost your mind? Ok, tell me the truth! What happened?" I questioned.

"Nothing."

"I don't believe that! Something has you talking like this. So tell me!"

"Ok, I spoke with one of my associates before you and Justice called. He told me that there are rumors floating around town that I'm loose. I don't want anyone thinking of me in that manner. Do you think I'm loose?" Kevyn asked with this I'm hurting look on his face.

I didn't want to make him feel any worse than he did, but the truth of the matter was that Kevyn was known for being a "ho." Who was I to judge? So, I decided to take the high road out.

"Kevyn, I must admit that I'm shocked that you of all people would allow something like that to bother you. You are one of the most secure people that I know."

"Dae'Mon, just answer the question."

"Kevyn, it's not a matter of what I think. It all boils down to what you like and no one else has a right to judge you for that. So what, if you like to sleep around! That's your business. As you put it, I keep my stuff on lock down. That's what I like to do. But it doesn't make me any better than anyone else."

"I guess you're right."

"I know I am, but to get back to what you asked me earlier as far as us dating again, I don't think so."

"Why?"

"We are too close to jeopardize our brotherhood."

"You're just afraid that I'm going to turn you out." Kevyn laughed.

"It's good to see you laugh. You had me worried there for a minute. But as far as you turning me out, I don't think so! It's been a while but I haven't lost my touch."

We laughed.

"My friend, thank you for keeping it real. I love you! Although, you know I'm not gay. I just prefer the company of a man."

We laughed.

CHAPTER SIX

Kevyn and I arrived at 12th and Hardesty at exactly 1:15 a.m. Justice was nowhere in sight. I was somewhat relieved although in the back of my mind I thought she would ambush us from behind a hidden bush. I laughed at the thought.

As Kevyn and I approached the small building, a line had formed in front of the door. Kevyn and I took our place in line with the rest of the kids who were waiting to get their party on.

The building where the party took place was a family diner that went under several years before. It provided the perfect setting for an intimate gathering such as this one. The building was beautifully decorated with Christmas lights in a variety of colors. The fluorescent colors of the lights made the building have a glow that could be seen for miles. It was truly something to behold.

Once we made it inside, the scene was off the hook. The music was blasting through the room, and the kids were feeling it! They were moving and grooving from every corner decorated in their New Year's get-ups. You know the type of outfits that scream for attention! Of course, I would never wear anything like that...Well at least I wouldn't admit it! Smile.

As Kevyn and I maneuvered through the building, all eyes were on him. He was thrilled that people were staring at him. He said that it made him feel important. I, on the other hand, felt like the homely boy who was always ignored. No one ever stared at me when I entered a room! Well, at least not the ones that I wanted to notice me!

I had a reputation of being stuck up cuz I didn't hang with the crowd, and I didn't allow just anyone to talk to me. I had never felt comfortable being a part of a clique.

Especially when they would cut each other down as a form of love- Junior High Schoolish!

Kevyn suggested that I get some dick, and I would loosen up. It had been a few years since I had sex, but Kevyn couldn't have been more wrong. I needed more than just a little orgasm here and there. Maybe I was weird, but I enjoyed spending quality time alone and hanging with a few choice friends. In my opinion, that didn't constitute one being stuck up. Anyway!

As we strolled through the room, Kevyn stopped to flirt with every guy he knew. I was getting annoyed cuz my hunger pains were screaming food, and I was trying to keep an eye out for Justice.

I was just about to nudge Kevyn until I noticed that he was engaged in conversation with Milton Parker. Kevyn had been after Milton for years and had yet to conquer him. The strange thing about it was that Milton had been after me for just as long.

Milton knew that Kevyn wanted him, but he didn't care. He stated on several occasions that he wanted me and not Kevyn. He referred to Kevyn as being free and open to the public. He went on to say that it would be a cold day in hell before he ever got with him. I didn't have the heart to tell Kevyn how Milton felt. Knowing Kevyn, he would have gotten mad and said that I was playa hating. Yeah if he only knew!

Under any other circumstances, I wouldn't have hesitated to go after Milton. However, I couldn't allow myself to get involved with him because Kevyn wanted him, and that violated one of my codes of friendship ethics. A friend should never get involved with a man that is liked, associated with, dated or had relations with a close friend. It could cause unnecessary friction. Sorry, no man was worth losing a friend over! Umm huh!

Truthfully speaking, Milton was very hot, and my temperature rose ten degrees higher just thinking about him.

He was dark skinned with a baldhead with muscles pouring out of every angle of his 6'2" 195 pound frame. He had a set of brown eyes that made me melt every time I looked at him.

In addition, Milton had great assets. He was a corporate lawyer, drove a BMW, had much cash and a condo to go along with the package. On top of it all, he was relationship oriented. Did you hear me? He wanted to settle down! Definitely my type of man! Any fool would have been pleased to have him. Just to think that he wanted me and I was running away from him like a fool!

I was not sure how much longer I could resist Milton. I purposely avoided him, and he purposely got in my face. He knew that I was weak, and he was waiting for the right moment to seal the deal. I forgot to mention Milton's voice. He had a deep rich baritone voice that was sexy and made me want to say, "Take me, take me now Milton!"

I know you're probably saying to yourself that I was a fool. Yeah, you're probably right!

Just as I was about to continue my lustful desire of Milton, I noticed Justice heading straight for us. She had a very angry look on her face, and I knew she was about to unload.

"Bring your lying ass here!" Justice said as she snatched me by the arm.

I noticed Milton watching me with a look of concern in his eyes. I was mesmerized although I knew Justice was about to give me hell.

"I thought you said Kevyn wasn't coming with you? What the fuck are you up to Dae'Mon?"

"First off, don't you use that tone with me! Secondly, you and Kevyn need to stop acting like little bitches and talk to each other." I snapped.

"You're the one playing these fucking games, Dae'Mon! I don't know why I put up with you and Kevyn. You bitches are trifling."

"I'm so sick of your tired ass attitude, Justice. You make me ill always getting an attitude every time you don't get your way. Now, you're going to take your damn ass over there and talk to Kevyn before I snatch you baldheaded."

I turned and walked away from her. She stood there in shock, just frozen in the spot where she was standing. She quickly regained her composure and walked over to where Kevyn and I were standing. Before she could say a word, I started talking.

"Kevyn, Justice would like to speak with you."

Kevyn rolled his eyes at me. He was livid that I would interrupt him while he was trying to get his mack on with Milton. Justice was standing there looking dumb that I had called her out. I was tired of their foolishness, so it was time for them to grow up. I walked to the nearest corner so I would not bear witness just in case they decided to kill one another.

From where I was standing, I could see that they were engaged in conversation. I was hoping they were putting their mess behind them. I also noticed that Milton was no longer standing there with Kevyn. Where could he be?

"Dae'Mon, how are you this evening?" the voice said from behind.

"I'm cool, thanks." I said as I turned to face Milton, as if I didn't recognize his voice. "Milton! What up?"

"Why were you being shady with me?"

"I wasn't being shady. You had your hands full with Kevyn and I didn't want to bother you." I said with a big smile.

"You could never bother me D! I'm hurt that you didn't acknowledge me." Milton said while pretending to cry.

"Don't even go there! You know I don't dip in Kevyn's business."

27

"Kevyn doesn't have any business with me. I've told you that too many times. When are you gonna let me wine and dine you?" Milton pleaded.

Milton's sexy voice was beginning to make my temperature rise, and I needed to get away from him before I ripped his clothes off, which was extremely difficult not to because the Levi's he was wearing made his ass look as tasty as a sweet potato pie. In addition, the tan pullover sweater he was wearing displayed every curve of his muscular frame.

"Well, Milton, if you will excuse me, I have to check on my friends." I said as I tried to make my getaway.

"Not so fast, Dae'Mon!" Milton said as he grabbed my arm. "I want to talk to you later and possibly dance with you, so don't even think about running off."

"I'm not going to do that! Milton, you know Kevyn would be mad."

"I don't give a damn about Kevyn! Understand? Do I have to spell it out for you? I'm interested in you Dae'Mon Greene! I'm tired of waiting." Milton said as he disappeared into the crowd before I could respond.

I began to fantasize about making love with Milton when Kevyn and Justice appeared.

"We made up!" Kevyn said.

"Well, I'm glad. You two can really work my damn nerves at times!" I snapped.

"What's eating you?" Justice questioned.

"Nothing, I'm just hungry."

"Well, we're sorry for acting up this evening!" she countered.

"Yeah, yeah, I'm hungry! Let's go to the kitchen." I said as I walked off.

I was happy that they made up, but I was mournful because I really wanted to spend the evening with Milton. I was allowing my fear of Kevyn's anger to keep me from a man that I should have been with years ago.

I had battled with this dilemma for years. I wanted Milton so bad that I could feel it. He was everything that I was looking for and more. I didn't think there was a better man in Kansas City than Milton Parker.

When all was said and done, could I truly say that Kevyn would refuse a man for me?

CHAPTER SEVEN

"Look at this shit!" I yelled.

Food was everywhere. The tables looked as if they had been invaded by a family of hungry grizzlies. The kids sure knew how to mess up a good thing.

Kevyn and Justice roared in laughter. I wasn't amused. I lost my appetite and wanted to leave, but Kevyn had other ideas. He looked around the room trying to find a reason to go on the prowl.

"What are we going to eat now?" I questioned.

"I'm going to the bathroom." Kevyn said.

"Kevyn, don't even try it! You are trying to run off to find Milton, aren't you?" I asked.

"I promise I'm not! I'm going to the bathroom and I'll be back in a zip."

"You know you're lying! That's cool though, I'll play along."

Kevyn left claiming he was headed to the bathroom. Justice and I both knew he was lying. Kevyn was in pursuit of a man and was not about to return anytime soon. He had played that game with us too many times before.

"Girl, you know Kevyn is lying?" I said.

"You didn't know? I hope you drove because we'll be lucky to see him again this evening. Remember the last time?"

We laughed. "Yeah, do I ever."

Kevyn was a pro at pulling a disappearing act. Justice and I went to a house party with him a few weeks before New Years. He went home with someone he met and left us there without saying a word. We had to find a ride home. Needless to say, we gave it to him with both barrels the next day. I knew he would probably pull a stunt like that again being that it was New Year's and all.

"Since it appears that I won't get anything to eat this evening, I guess I'll have a drink." I said.

"Ooh, would you get me one?" Justice asked.

"Why can't you go with me?"

"I see someone at the bar that I don't like. Please! I want a Vodka and cranberry." Justice begged.

"Likely story, you'll probably run off too!"

"I promise I won't. I'm not Kevyn remember?"

"Ok, I'll be right back." I said as headed to the bar.

As I approached the counter, I noticed a very attractive man serving drinks. I was in awe. It didn't help the cause with him not wearing a shirt. He was about 6'0" 175 pounds with muscles just vibrating with every movement of his body. I was getting very aroused staring at him. Can you believe that? Twice in one night!

"What can I get for you sweetheart?" the bartender said.

I wanted to say how about you naked in my bed, but I refrained from embarrassing myself.

"I'll have a Vodka and Cranberry and an Amarillo Sour." I responded.

"Speak up, sweetheart! I can't hear you."

"I'll have a VODKA AND CRANBERRY AND AMARILLO SOUR, PLEASE!" I repeated.

"Not so loud! I'm not wearing a miracle ear." He said with a smile.

"I wanted to make sure you could hear me." I said as embarrassment filled my body.

"So, what's your name?" he questioned.

"Dae'Mon."

"It's a pleasure to serve you Dae'Mon. I'm Jamal."

He had a dimple to go along with his beautiful smile. I was falling in love each time my eyes blinked. I wanted to have his baby. I wanted to drink his bath water. Simply put, Jamal was ovah! You hear me?

"The pleasure is all mine." I said trying to compose myself, all the while undressing him with my eyes.

31

"You like what you see?" he asked.

"What are you talking about?" I said trying to play dumb.

"Come off of it! I see how you're lusting over me." He said with a coy grin on his face.

"Whatever! My drinks please!"

"Only if you promise to give me your number!"

"Why?"

"I wanna take you out to dinner."

"For what reason?"

"I think you're cute, and I want to get to know you better! Give a brotha a chance to show you how a real man operates!

"Yeah right! You're probably a playboy trying to see how many number you can collect tonight." I responded.

"I don't play games. I'm a real man So, are you gonna give me your number or not?" He questioned.

"What the hell!" I said.

I wrote my number on a napkin that was lying on the bar and gave it to him. I was more than thrilled to give him the digits, and I was not ashamed to say that was not all I wanted to give him. Shut up! You would have done the same thing too. I was equally impressed with him giving me his number without me having to ask for it. Believe it or not, he gave me his home number and not a beepa number. I hate that!

I skipped back over to where Justice was standing. I had a smile on my face as wide as Texas.

"Dae'Mon Greene! What are you up to?" Justice said suspiciously while taking her drink from my hand.

"Nothing!" I said giggling like a teenage schoolgirl.

"I don't believe you. I saw you over there getting cozy with that bartender. He's a hottie."

"He's a ten piece and a biscuit."

We laughed.

"Kevyn is going to hate you for getting to him first."

"Whatever! It's not like Jamal is Kevyn's man."

"Jamal." Justice repeated. "On a first name basis already. I'm scared of you!"

"It's not like I'm going to marry him. He just wants to take me out for dinner."

"If you say so. Child, a man that looks like that is only after one thing."

"And just what is that, Mother Justice?"

Kevyn was right! Justice always tried to cock block. Maybe if she had gotten herself a man, she would have stopped hating on me.

"All I'm saying is to be careful and don't get your hopes up that he's going to be the one." She countered.

"Did you hear me say anything like that? Girl, I swear you would drive a crazy man sane! I'm gonna find Kevyn. Uh!" I said as I walked away.

Justice stood there looking dumb as if she had no clue what was going on. She was still bitter after being dumped by her man that she had been with for five years. It seemed that she was on a mission to make everyone become a card-carrying member of her "I Hate Men Club." In her case, straight men! She could go on hating men, but I was not singing that tune anymore. It was a New Year, and I was going to fall in love again. I found a spot near the dance floor; and just when I thought it couldn't get any worse, I saw Milton approaching me.

"What's up D? How about that dance?" he smiled."

"I don't recall agreeing to dance with you."

"You don't have a choice."

"The hell I don't!" I retorted.

"Dae'Mon, I have waited for you for a long time, and it's time for you to let go of your fears. I know you want to be with me. I can see it in your beautiful eyes. So, stop worrying about Kevyn and do what your heart is telling you to do!" He said as he gently massaged my arm.

Not even my quick-wits could get me out of that one! Milton was right. It was my fear keeping me from him, but what about Kevyn? I didn't know what to do, so I stood there in silence.

"What? Cat got your tongue?" he questioned.

"Milton, you just don't understand…"

"What's there to understand Dae'Mon? You want to be with me and you know it! Stop fooling yourself and let me love you and no I don't mean sexually either." Milton said as he cut me off in mid sentence.

I was near tears. I just couldn't betray my friendship with Kevyn. Not even Milton Parker, Mr. Debonair himself, could make me jeopardize that! It was easier for me to go after Jamal cuz as far as I knew he was single. Well at least I hoped he was since he asked me out!

"Dae'Mon, don't stand there like you don't hear me!"

"I heard you loud and clear Milton."

"Aren't you going to say something?" Milton said with a quizzical look on his face.

"Like what?" I snapped.

Before I knew it, Milton had grabbed me and began to passionately kiss my lips. The kiss was so powerful and intense that it sent sparks through my body. I was on fire and about to lose control. I wanted to stop him, but I was unable to do so. I pushed against his chest trying to part our lips but to no avail. The harder I pushed the more ravenously he kissed me exploring my mouth like a starved tiger devouring its' prey. I finally stopped resisting and melted into his arms. I was loving every minute of the symphonic thrill his tongue sent down my quivering spine. I felt as if we were the only two people in the world. The crowd of people around us had become invisible at least in my eyesight. My head was suddenly spinning out of control and I felt my love juice about to explode in my pants.

"Bitch! What the fuck are you doing?"

I opened my eyes to find Kevyn standing in front of us. His stare scolding us for the sinful act we had just committed. I became warm all over and felt embarrassed. How could I have done such a thing? I was angry with myself. I was in disbelief.

"My God what have I done?" I cried out.

"You know what the fuck you've done? You ain't nothing but a skank ass ho!" Kevyn screamed with his hands on his hips.

"You're the whore, bitch!" Milton yelled pointing his finger at Kevyn.

"Milton, stop it!' I said trying to calm the scene.

"Stop what bitch! You need to stop it! You fucking ho!

Before I knew it, Kevyn's face came into contact with the back of my hand. The force of my hand hitting his face was so great, it knocked him on his butt. He quickly rose to his feet.

A large crowd had begun to encircle us. The kids always loved a good fight, and Kevyn's dumb ass was giving them one for no reason whatsoever.

"Dae'Mon, you ain't shit! You ain't shit, you fucking bitch! I'm gonna fuck you up!" Kevyn said as he rushed towards me.

"You're not going to do shit to him bitch!" Milton said as he jumped in front of me. I was in a daze and lost for words. I didn't know what to say to rectify the situation. I looked around for a way out, but couldn't find a hole to jump in. Justice came to save the day. She ran from the back of the room almost tripping over her own feet.

She gulped down her drink.

"Alright, Kevyn! That's enough! You're embarrassing yourself. Let's go!" Justice said.

"Yeah, let's go. I can't stand looking at that dirty bitch one more minute. I'll get his ass later." Kevyn said.

"Take your tired ass on Kevyn! You're nothing but trash with yo bitch ass!" Milton screamed as Kevyn and Justice walked out of the building.

I stood there frozen in place overcome by the guilt and embarrassment that had befallen on me. I was confused and not sure of my surroundings anymore until Milton wrapped his arm around my waist and led me outside.

"I'm sorry baby! I don't k now what the fuck Kevyn was thinking!" Milton stated.

"Please just take me home! I need to be alone right now!" I said.

"Ok baby, let's go! ...Dae'Mon, everything will work out for this best. I just hope you can believe that!" Milton said as he looked into my eyes.

After a brief silence, Milton led me to his car.

CHAPTER EIGHT

What a night?

I never thought I would live to see the day when I would lose a friend over a man, especially when the man and the friend were not in a relationship. It didn't make sense! Kevyn knew that he could never have Milton. That was probably why he became so enraged. Remember in his eyes, I was like the ugly stepsister who didn't get any play; but this time, I was the one who ran off with the prize. How dare me? No, how dare Kevyn blow up at me for no good reason? Was I not good enough to have a good-looking man like Milton? Did I deserve to have only trashy men in my life? I didn't think so! I deserved only the very best, and I showed him that I was not giving in to his little temper tantrum.

"Dae'Mon, are you ok?" Milton said as he placed his hand on my upper thigh.

"Milton, please remove your hand and yes I'm fine. I'm just thinking about what a shitty night this has turned out to be."

"It's not your fault! Kevyn is the one who made an ass of himself over nothing. He knows that I don't want him, and he doesn't want you to have me either."

"But Milton, if you had just left well enough alone, I wouldn't be in this predicament."

Milton rolled his eyes. "Why Dae'Mon? You have been fighting your feelings for years. For what? Just so Kevyn wouldn't get angry with you. That's really fucked up! What type of friend would try to keep another friend from being happy! Can you explain that? He's supposed to be your homeboy, but he treats you like shit and you allow him to do so! When are you going to open your eyes and realize that Kevyn doesn't care about anyone other than himself?"

"That's a lie! That's a damn lie! He was there when I was depressed, and no one else was there for emotional support. Thanks to him I no longer feel empty inside! He has become my family and I will always love him for that!" I yelled.

"Oh yeah! How long are you going to pay that price? Because if you ask me, the bill is too damn expensive?"

"Well, no one asked you! How dare you sit here and try to tell me about my friend. You don't know him. You don't know me for that matter! So who in the fuck gave you the right to make a judgment call on something you know absolutely nothing about?"

"Dae'Mon, you are one of the sweetest guys that I know, but you are so naïve. You have no idea as to what's been going on do you?" Milton questioned.

"What are you talking about, Milton?"

"I'm talking about the things that your so called best friend, Kevyn, has been up to lately!"

"What are you getting at?" I questioned, suddenly feeling like I was about to walk into an ambush at the Alamo.

"Well, did Mr. Kevyn tell you that he came over to my house and wanted me to fuck him? Did he tell you that he badmouthed you to me? Did he tell you that he slept with my friend, Alonzo, to get back at me? Of course he didn't?"

"Milton, get off of it? You're just saying that because of what happened tonight. Stop trying to save face!"

"You know what Dae'Mon, I've just about had enough of this! I'm not going to run after you anymore! If you want to continue being friends with that trifling no good for nothing, then be my guest! But don't ever say that I didn't warn you! He's a snake and he's going to continue to keep you down as long as you let him. You need to open your eyes to see what type of friend Kevyn really is. If you don't, you are going to live a very lonely life. Kevyn will never allow you to be happy with me or anyone else for that matter! He is jealous of you Dae'Mon! Open your eyes before it's too late!"

With that said, Milton pulled over to the curb in front of my building. I could tell that he was fuming. I could see the hurt in his eyes, but I was so confused. I didn't know what to do or what to say. I just sat there waiting for someone to rescue me. No one did! So, I had to face my demons alone and give thought to everything Milton said. Could there be some truth to it? I knew one way to find out for sure, Justice. She would be more than happy to sing like a canary.

"So, I guess this is it, huh?" Milton questioned me with what seemed to be tears in his eyes.

"Milton, I just don't know what I'm thinking right now. I'm so confused. My heart is telling me to snatch you up because I probably won't meet another man of your caliber again, but my mind is telling me to run. I know you probably don't understand where I'm coming from, but you have to believe me when I say that I'm completely at a loss."

I rubbed his baldhead with my hand trying to provide comfort to him. I wanted to just lose myself in his arms again, but I was too afraid. His sad puppy dog eyes were doing a number on me. I turned away from him to avoid his gaze.

"Dae'Mon." Milton said while placing his hand on my shoulder. "I know it's not easy. There is a lot at stake, but believe me when I say that it's the right thing to do."

I stared out the window at the sky not wanting to deal with the situation at hand.

"Milton, I just can't." I said as tears welled up in my eyes.

"Dae'Mon, look at me!"

Milton began to pull me over to him. I didn't resist. I moved closer. Milton put his hand around my chin and looked directly into my eyes.

"Dae'Mon, the last thing I want to do is hurt you. I only want to love you like you deserve to be loved. You deserve that and much more. I know you're a special person because I keep hearing you talk about Kevyn's feelings and not once have you mentioned anything about how you feel. I want you to realize that your happiness is what's most important. You have to live your life for yourself and not worry about how others are going to react to you and that includes Kevyn. He is just going have to get use to us being together." Milton said as he gently kissed my lips.

"Milton, I can't." I said as the tears began to freely roll down my face.

"Only because you don't want it to happen! It's time for you to follow your heart and stop worrying about Kevyn."

I began to sob uncontrollably as I buried my face in Milton's chest. He held me tightly as he rubbed the back of my neck.

"Just let it go, baby! Let it go!" Milton said.

Why was I crying? It was for one particular reason. I was crying because for the first time in five years I was about to allow someone to love me.

When I finally stopped crying, Milton lifted me up from his chest and began to dry my face with a napkin. He had a million-dollar smile on his face, which was priceless. I suddenly became embarrassed just thinking about the scene I had put on.

"Milton, I'm so sorry. I didn't mean to…"

"There is no need to explain, Dae'Mon. You needed to do that for all the things that you have been through. Now, you have opened the door to the future." He said as he suddenly kissed my left cheek.

"You're right, Milton. I'm just so afraid though."

"I know, but we can deal with it together. I know Kevyn is an issue for you, but I don't want you to deal with him alone. I'm the reason he's angry, and we'll solve it together. Ok?"

"Yes, I understand. I just hope that I'm making the right decision." I said as I buried my face in my hands. I could feel the tears flowing again.

"You are making the right decision Dae'Mon! I'm not going to allow anyone to hurt you anymore. Come here!"

Milton wiped my tears away again as I looked into his eyes. I wondered what he was thinking at that moment. He was probably saying what a nut!

"Milton, it's getting late. I think it's time for us to go to bed." I said as I grabbed his hand.

"I know that's my cue to leave."

"No, I don't want you to leave. I want to lie in your arms all night. I just need you here with me right now."

"Ok, if you insist." Milton grinned.

"Don't play like you don't want to Milton Parker!"

"I promise I'll be on my best behavior."

"Yeah, I know you will. I'm not even worried. Now, let's go inside unless you want to sleep out here?"

"Ok, but no funny stuff!"

I laughed. "Milton!"

Milton shut the car off and climbed out as I was putting on my coat. To my surprise, he walked around to open the door for me. I felt like a celebrity. We headed inside the building from the cold night air. As I was unlocking the door, Milton grabbed me from behind by my waist and kissed me on the back of the neck. He pulled away with a big grin on his face like he had done something amazing. I turned my head to look at him.

"You were supposed to be on your best behavior, Dae'Mon!"

We laughed and entered my loft.

CHAPTER NINE

Sweet kisses in the morning time…

I was awakened by the sensation of tender kisses being planted on my forehead. I could feel the sparks vibrating through my body at a rapid pace like that of a lightening storm. I was truly flying on Cloud 9 at that moment, and I knew it was only going to be a matter of time before my lovetool would betray me. I felt it stiffening, so I jumped out of bed and ran to the bathroom. I wasn't ready for sex with Milton as of yet. I wanted to make sure we got to know each other first before we crossed that line because once it had been crossed there was no turning back.

When I came out of the bathroom, Milton was lying on my queen size bed with a big grin on his face. His beautiful smile was turning me on. I was feeling a stiff one coming on again, so I had to escape from the trance he was putting me under. Otherwise, I knew that I would attack him like a sex-starved maniac. It had been five years since I did the grownup!

"Milton sweetheart, what would you like for breakfast?" I asked as I tried to find my robe to conceal my joy, if you catch my drift!

"I want you baby! Come here!" Milton said with a hint of seduction in his eyes.

I knew if I went over to him I would lose control. I tried to play it off by appearing to clean the night- stand.

"What's the matter Dae'Mon? You afraid of little old me?" He said with a sly grin.

"No, I'm making sure my house is clean. The maid is off this week." I said avoiding his eyes.

"Please!" He laughed. "Come here, baby!"

"What do you want Milton?"

"Come over here and find out!"

"In a minute after I fix breakfast." I said trying to leave the room.

Milton jumped out of bed and grabbed me from behind. I could feel his erection throbbing against my back. I knew I wouldn't be able to resist at that point.

Milton began kissing the back of my neck with his soft lips as he massaged my erect nipples. I could feel my body temperature rise as it ached from desire. As Milton's soft lips massaged my skin with each kiss, my lovetool started coming to life. I wanted to put a stop to it until we had a chance to talk, but my body was saying otherwise.

I closed my eyes and laid my head back as Milton took my robe off and began to kiss the back of my spine. I shrieked with delight. His tongue made my body tingle with every stroke. He gently rubbed my chest as I moaned from his touch. It was too good, and I couldn't take anymore.

"Milton, we shouldn't." I said through my heavy breathing.

"Baby, just relax!" Milton said as he pulled my Calvin Klein boxers down to my ankles.

He let his tongue slide down my back until it came to the base of my buttocks. He slowly massaged my cheeks exploring every inch of its' shape. I wanted to explode. I turned around and pulled him up to me. I began to devour his lips like a ripened strawberry.

"Day-am baby! Your lips are wicked." Milton said coming up for air.

I was feeling it and wasn't about to stop. I slowly slid Milton's Ralph Lauren underwear to the floor. I went for his lips again as our bodies bumped and grind to the beat of our own tune. I made my way to his neck where I attacked with a vengeance. It was as if I was a vampire trying to draw blood. He moaned and groaned as I tickled his neck with my moist tongue. I began to caress his muscular chest with one hand and palmed his plump juicy ass with the other.

"Dae'Mon, you're bad!" He said in between his moaning.

"I'm bad! I'll show you just how bad I am." I said as I grabbed him around the waist and forcefully pushed him on the bed.

Milton looked helpless. I smiled as I zeroed in on his tempting nipples making him scream out my name. "Dae'Mon!" I sucked and gently bit his nipples as his body shook and swiveled from the excitement. He was moving about like he was possessed with demon hounds from hell. I was enjoying every bit of it.

He stroked the back of my head as I navigated my way around his body purposely avoiding the mid-section. I had something very special in mind for that big boy. What can I say? Milton was blessed. Long and thick! Ouch!

I grabbed Milton by his waist and flipped him onto his stomach. I dragged my tongue from the base of his neck until I reached the bull's-eye. I was being greedy and couldn't stop. I worked his ass like barbecue on a chicken. He screamed out in obscenities.

"Damn Dae'Mon! Yeah, baby! Eat it! Hell Yeah! Fuck Yeah! Oooh, Oooh!"

The more he talked, the more I worked it on him. I licked, sucked, blew and gently chewed every nestle of his hole. He was weak, and I was just getting started. His hip movement was in synch with every lick. I got a little too excited and slapped his ass, which made him jump. I didn't know I had it in me. Scandalous! I could tell he didn't like being spanked by the look he shot me.

"Sorry, Baby! I got a little carried away." I said as I continued to devour his tasty treat before he could say a word.

I flipped him on his back again and descended straight to his family jewel. I teased him by licking from the shaft to the head. When he shriveled, I would stop.

"Day-am baby! Don't stop! Please!" Milton begged.

I went all the way down on it and almost gagged. He loved it, but I couldn't breathe. I caught my breath and starting sucking it like there was no tomorrow. He squirmed and screamed.

"Fuck yeah, Dae'Mon! Suck it, baby! Yeah!"

I was supercharged like the Energizer Bunny after that. I sucked it like a melting ice cream cone on a hot summer day. I was overcome with the sensation of wanting to see him explode, so I stayed down on it like a jackhammer. He couldn't take anymore. He grabbed the back of my head and was shaking uncontrollably.

"Damn baby! Shit, you really sucking that bad boy. Oooh! Please don't stop!"

I wanted to laugh, but I still had work to do. I came up for air and did a swan dive back to the prize with enough force to rock a small building. He loved it. He began to speak in tongue, and I was speaking in dick.

"Dae'Mon, I'm gonna cum! I'm gonna cum!" He screamed.

I raised up just in time. He exploded all over his chest, the wall and the bedding. He was shaking violently and still speaking in an unknown language. I just sat back with a huge grin on my face enjoying the view. It took five minutes for him to stop shaking. His eyes opened.

"Damn baby! Were you making up for lost time? That was off the chain!" He said still trying to catch his breath.

"That was nothing." I said grinning.

"That was a ten piece and biscuit."

We laughed.

"Speaking of, what do you want for breakfast?" I asked as I tried to get up from the bed.

"Just where do you think you're going?" Milton said as he pulled me on top of him.

"Milton, Yuk!" I said as I got his man-juice all over me.

He grabbed a towel and cleaned the mess we had made. He then jumped on top of me.

"It's your turn." He said as he started nibbling my neck.

I was now the one squirming as he explored the vicinity of my entire body with his tongue. He began to concentrate on my nipples, which were now very aroused and begging for attention. He didn't disappoint either! He tickled my nipples with the tip of his tongue, which shot bolts through my body. I was screaming in pure delight.

"Work that tongue, baby!"

My nipples felt like tiny electrical storms. The sparks were driving me crazy and I couldn't take anymore. I grabbed his head and brought his face up to mine and passionately kissed his luscious lips. He pulled back and went to work on my legs. He started with my knees. Just sucking and licking! I was surprised that my knees were very sensitive. I enjoyed the sensation of his lips next to my skin. He traveled up to my inner thighs where he had me in convulsions. I squealed from his touch. I was just beginning to shake when he picked me up and sat me on his face. He explored my ripped love-canal like it had never been done before.

"Milton, please stop! I can't take it! Please stop!" I yelled.

It was as if Milton didn't hear me. He continued to eat me out like a ravenous beast. He was simply mad I tell you. He flipped me over, placing me on all fours. He nose-dived into my prize with a force that sent his tongue through the opening. I screamed.

"Milton! Please stop, please! Oh damn baby! Stop!"

I tried to crawl away, but he grabbed me by the back of the neck and pulled me to him. He locked his arm around my stomach to keep me from moving, and he licked and chewed and licked and sucked and blew and blew. I was about to pass out from the joy I was receiving.

"You like that shit, don't you baby?" He said as he grabbed a quick breath only to dive in again.

"Oh Milton! Yes, baby! Eat it! Eat it, Milton!"

My breathing was now very heavy and I was having heart palpitations. I was under a trance and wanted more. Milton again didn't disappoint. He flipped me over on my back and went for my nipples again. I began to shake and tried to push him off of me. He held me down with one hand as he massaged my lovetool. I was squirming and moaning so loud I was sure the neighbors could here me.

"Shit baby! I can't take anymore…Stop…no…no"

Milton ignored my plea and went down on me. He swallowed me whole. My breath stopped.

"Oooh…Oooh…yeah Milton! Suck it! Suck it good baby!"

He slipped, slid and slobbered all over my erection. I was shaking uncontrollably now and wanted to explode. He returned my jackhammer favor and massaged my lovetool with his hand while pulsating up and down at the same time. This feeling sent me through the roof.

"Baby, I can't hold it any longer!" I whispered.

He swallowed me whole one last time and removed his mouth as I shot off like a raging volcano spewing lava over the town. It took over a minute before I finally stop shooting off my man-juice.

I could tell Milton was pleased with himself with the cheshire grin on his face. I didn't have enough energy to move, so I just laid there in my afterglow. Milton grabbed a towel and cleaned me up. We had ruined the comforter. I was gonna have to do laundry big time.

"You liked that baby?" Milton asked as he laid on top of me.

"Yes, very much so!" I responded breathlessly.

"Good, I'm glad you enjoyed yourself!"

We kissed.

CHAPTER TEN

How do I describe my morning with Milton?

I think one word could sum it up. Simply Incredible! That was two words, but you can imagine what I was feeling at the time. I felt like a brand new person. I broke down walls that had stood firm for years. I was headed in a positive direction and looked forward to starting a new life with Milton. I was finally free and no longer afraid.

As happy as I was, I needed to have a major discussion with Milton. I was afraid because I didn't know how he was going to react to me. I thought to myself that if I could get through a bout of depression I could probably get through anything.

"Milton, breakfast was great! I didn't know you had it in you." I said smiling.

"There's a lot I got in me. If you play your cards right, I might let you find out the rest."

"Yeah I bet!"

I walked over to the sofa where Milton was sitting and plopped down on his lap. He had a classic smile on his face that made me just want to eat him up. Instead, I nibbled on his ear, and he squealed like a pig. I felt warm all over being with him.

"Baby, did you enjoy this morning?" Milton asked as he rubbed my backside.

I raised up from my nibbling. "The breakfast, you mean?" I knew he wasn't talking about the meal.

He slapped me on the ass and said, "You know I'm not talking about breakfast!"

I jumped when his hand connected with on my derriere. I could feel myself getting titillated again. I thought about the discussion Milton and I needed to have so I removed myself from his lap before things got heated again.

"Milton, I know we have crossed that line, but I need to know something, not that it would matter now though. But have you been tested?"

"Tested for what? Are you trying to tell me something?" Milton said with a quizzical look on his face.

"No, I'm not trying to tell you anything. I was just a little concerned cuz I allowed myself to get caught up in the moment without asking first." I responded.

"Come here, baby!" Milton said as he motioned for me with his hand.

I walked over to Milton and sat on his lap. "Milton, I'm trying to have a serious discussion."

He ignored my statement and began to passionately kiss me. I was lost in the moment and enjoying the touch of his lips pressed against mine.

I was embarrassed that I even brought up the subject. What was I thinking? Milton was a prominent attorney. He couldn't have possibly been sick. Besides, he looked perfectly healthy to me I thought to myself. I felt that I worried too much. That was my problem.

"Baby, I need to take a shower." Milton said between kisses.

"Only if I can get in there with you?" I said, and then slid my tongue down his throat.

Milton had lips that tasted like juicy peaches. I felt like those people in the Big Red Commercials, just kiss a little longer. Milton didn't realize that he could get anything just by kissing me. As the song by SWV goes I Get So Weak...

Milton pulled back and looked into my eyes. He gently stroked my face. "Dae'Mon Greene, you have made me the happiest man in the world."

"No, I'm the happiest man in the world, and I look forward to spending the rest of my days on earth with you. Thank you Milton!"

"For what?" he questioned.

"For not giving up on me. I was so confused. But I have found my way now!" I smiled.

"Dae'Mon, I wanted you the moment I first laid eyes on you three years ago. I wasn't about to give up that easily."

"Stop lying, Milton!" I said as I tweaked his nose.

"I'm serious. I was in awe when I saw you, and I was sad to see you with Kevyn."

"Why is that?"

"I knew Kevyn was trash and hoped that you weren't dating him. I had to have you, and it hurt me that you didn't even acknowledge my presence."

"Milton, Kevyn and I went out on one date. He was too high maintenance for me, so we decided to become friends."

Milton's eyes grew larger, not believing what he was hearing. I freaked out and began to explain without Milton uttering a word.

"Milton, you don't have to worry. I never had sex with Kevyn. I wasn't ready for it and believe it or not, he never pressured me." I said nervously.

He kissed my forehead and placed his arm around my waist. "I'm not worried about that Dae'Mon. I'm just surprised that's all."

"You have to admit that Kevyn is attractive? Come on, Milton!" I responded.

"He is, but I heard about Kevyn before I ever met him."

"What do you mean?"

Milton looked at me as if I had committed a cardinal sin. It was almost as if he was in disbelief that I didn't know what he was talking about.

"Dae'Mon, I was told that if I wanted a good fuck to look up Kevyn Howard. I know at least ten people who said they had him and that's why I have never respected him."

I was beginning to get angry. I heard the same rumors about Kevyn when I first met him. Even though, I never stopped loving him. He was my friend, and I would always stand by him. So what if he liked to have sex with a lot of people! That didn't make any of us better than him. To each his own!

"Can we talk about something else, please?" I asked.

"Of course baby! Back to you though! I asked a lot of people about you. No one had a bad thing to say. I made a promise to myself then that one day we would be together."

I gave Milton a big kiss. "You're making me blush!"

"It's the truth. Dae'Mon you have class written all over you and I can't think of another person in this city like you. I'm glad you didn't find anyone else. You know you were saving yourself for me. Admit it!" Milton laughed as he began to tickle me.

I kicked and screamed trying to free myself from Milton's grasp. I finally wrestled myself loose only to end up on the floor. I quickly rose to my feet and straddled Milton's lap.

"Milton, I wasn't ready for you back then; and when I found myself ready, Kevyn's attraction to you stood in my way. I have to admit that I have longed for your touch for a while now. And there were times I would see you out and curse myself for being a coward."

"You had it bad, didn't you?" Milton said as he broke out in boisterous laughter.

I couldn't do anything but laugh at Milton. He was enjoying the moment and so was I. I didn't think I could ever feel that good about another person after the past two relationships I had. I gave up on love and never knew it was right under my nose.

"Don't get mad, but I thought you were a playboy when I first saw you. You know I was given the full run down on you, but I was more smitten with your sex appeal. I had many fantasies about you."

Milton's eyes bulged when I mentioned what I thought of him. I could tell that he was flattered.

"You really did like me? Wow, I thought you hated the ground I walked on. You were always so cold and distant towards me."

"It was only because I liked you and didn't want Kevyn to know, so I had to play that 'I hate you" role. I'm sorry I should have been stronger to go after what I wanted."

"Don't' be sorry! The important thing is we're together now." Milton said as he kissed me on the lips.

"Amen my brother! Say that!" I said as our lips parted.

Milton flipped me over on my back and climbed on top of me. He began to slowly kiss my neck and suddenly made his way to my awaiting lips. I moaned as our lips connected. The kiss was soft and sweet. I could feel my lovetool stiffening as my body begged for Milton's touch. Milton pulled my robe from around my shoulders and tenderly kissed every spot on my upper body. I jumped with every feel of his lips on my skin. I was slowly rising to ecstasy and felt myself coming close to a climax. Milton must have sensed it probably because my moaning became louder and my breathing became heavier. He removed my underwear with the precision of a surgeon's knife. He rose to his feet and removed his clothing with one stroke.

He picked me up and gently placed me on the floor. He laid on top of me and our lips were drawn to each other like strong magnets. This time the kiss was more forceful but still burned with passion. Milton began to massage my nipples with the tip of his fingers as he nibbled on my ear.

I cried out, "Milton, baby! I'm gonna…I'm gonna explode."

"Me too." He whispered.

As if our bodies were synchronized, we erupted into bliss at the same time. It was pure joy. Just beautiful! It had been a long time since I enjoyed sex. Milton laid on top of me trying to catch his breath. I was trying to catch my breath and Milton's weight bearing down on me didn't help matters. We laid there for what seemed like an eternity enjoying the moment before Milton finally got up and walked into the bathroom.

"Damn! Baby, you should be ashamed of what you did." Milton said laughing.

"Me? This was all of your doing. You took advantage of me." I said with a straight face.

"You're too much! Anyway, let's get in the shower before we go at it again."

Milton turned on the water to the shower and hopped in. I climbed in behind him.

The water permeated our bodies as we melted into each other's arms.

CHAPTER ELEVEN

After Milton left, I sat around thinking about what had transpired earlier that morning at the party. It brought tears to my eyes that Kevyn would be so willing to give up our friendship simply because he couldn't get what he wanted. How many times does a person have to say I'm not interested, before it sinks in? He knew he didn't have a snowballs chance in hell of ever getting Milton, but that didn't stop him from trying and blowing up at me because I was Milton's choice.

I was beginning to doubt my friendship with Kevyn. It appeared to me to be a friendship of convenience. His convenience! I loved him dearly because he stuck beside me when I was down and that was not an easy task. But as Milton put it, how long did I have to pay the price? As time passed, he would only call me when he wanted something or wanted company when he couldn't get in touch with one of his tricks. I was beginning to believe that he was jealous. However, there were times when I wanted to be like him.

He was the life of every party. Everyone loved his energy, and they would crowd around him no matter where he was. I was labeled snooty because I wouldn't sleep with everyone. Well, I was not a doorknob where everybody got a turn! Furthermore, I wasn't the type that socialized with just anyone. You lay down with dogs; you'll get up with fleas! Kevyn always had a positive outlook on life, and he had gotten everything that he wanted. Well, not everything-Milton! I think that rejection was what caused him to pursue Milton in the manner he did for three years. Milton was a major challenge, and Kevyn was not going out like that.

When he saw Milton and I kissing, his ego was deflated. He viewed it as a slap in the face. His best defense was to cause a scene that would in turn embarrass me and make me run for the border. It didn't work out that way. I ended up with the prize after all. Can you believe that?

I have witnessed Kevyn do some ruthless things to people to get back at them. For example, he went out with this guy named Maurice. Kevyn wanted Maurice to buy him a living room set. When he refused, Kevyn called the guy's mother and told her that Maurice was gay. Maurice came after Kevyn with a vengeance. Justice and I put our lives at risk trying to protect Kevyn from him. Maurice pulled a gun on Kevyn one night at Connections. I begged and pleaded to Maurice to not shoot Kevyn. I was grateful when he listened.

After all that, I still stood beside him. I had been a better friend to him than he had been to me. You would think that he would have been happy for me. It had been five years since I was in a relationship. He was the one who always told me to get over it and allow someone to love me. When I did, he got angry. Go figure!

I decided that I would make an attempt to rectify the situation. So I called Kevyn to discuss the incident.

I dialed his number. I tapped the end of my fingers on the table as I waited for an answer.

"Hello," Kevyn said after the third ring.

"Hello, Kevyn. This is Dae'Mon." I responded.

"What the hell do you want?" Kevyn snapped.

"I called to apologize for hitting you. I didn't mean to. You were saying some cruel things, and I lost my head for a moment."

"Dae'Mon, I really don't want to talk to you right now. You're not the friend I thought you were."

I rolled my eyes. "Kevyn, you're my best friend. We need to work through this." I said as I stood up and began pacing back and forth.

"Dae'Mon, I just can't believe you would embarrass me the way you did at the party. You knew that I wanted Milton, but you went after him anyway. I have seen the lust in your eyes whenever he was around, but I never thought you would stoop that low."

"I apologize if you feel that I embarrassed you. But, if anyone is embarrassed it's me. Now, Kevyn, please be realistic! You have known for years that Milton has wanted to go out with me, but I refused to date him because of you."

"Oh really! You certainly had a hard time refusing him this time. What in the hell do you call what you were doing last night? Friendly conversation?" Kevyn questioned in a hostile tone.

"Milton simply kissed me."

"So, you didn't kiss him back?"

"Yes I did. I couldn't resist this time. I had been fighting my feelings for him for a long time and last night I wasn't strong enough to refuse him."

I could hear Kevyn clapping his hands. "And the Oscar goes to Dae'Mon Greene for best performance in a kissing scene. Give me a fucking break, Dae'Mon! You just didn't want me to have Milton. That's it plain and simple!" Kevyn yelled.

"I'm truly sorry that you feel that way. I didn't know I was going to see Milton last night. It was your idea to go to the party in the first place. You know what Kevyn? You're being very selfish here! You should be happy that I'm dating someone." I countered.

"That's fucking great! You have a lot of nerve calling me selfish! I stood by your tired ass when you were depressed. I put up with your endless whining for months. I was there when your own family wasn't around and you have the nerve to call me selfish. Well, fuck you Dae'Mon Greene."

"Alright that's it! I have had about enough of this as I'm gonna take. You don't have to be so nasty…"

"You didn't have to be a back-stabbing bitch either, but you are!"

"The last time I checked, you and Milton were not dating. As a matter of fact, you know he didn't want you!"

"Yeah, cuz you had your trifling ass waiting in the wing for the right moment to steal him from me."

I laughed. "You gotta be fucking kidding. So, I'm trifling now. That's a compliment coming from someone who uses men like wet wipes."

"You're just jealous cuz nobody wants you, bitch."

"Well, Milton does."

"So fucking what? He's a ho just like you."

"Coming from a person who has slept with almost every man in the State of Missouri, I kindly accept that as a compliment."

"I'm through talking to yo ass. Fuck you and don't call my house anymore!"

I froze in my tracks. "You ain't got to worry about that. You bitter mothafucker! Fuck you! Stupid bitch!" I said as I slammed the phone down.

I could not believe my ears. Kevyn actually accused me of stealing Milton from him. Before that could happen, don't the two people have to be involved? Yeah, that's what I thought!

I had endured his lack of maturity for years. He never took ownership for his own actions. It was always someone else's fault in his eyes. After all, he was Mr. Perfect. He could never do any wrong and always had everyone's best interest in mind. Yeah right!

Even if I had stolen Milton from Kevyn (which I didn't), it would have served him right. Get a load of this! There was this guy named Shawn Jones. Shawn had a thing for me and pursued me like Milton did. He would call me all the time, and Kevyn was at my house during several of those phone calls. Anyway, Shawn left a message on my answering machine one night inviting me out to dinner. I never got the message because Kevyn took it upon himself to listen to my messages while I was in the shower. Do you know he had the nerve to show up at the restaurant? What made it worse was the fact that Kevyn told Shawn that I didn't like him and didn't want to talk to him anymore.

Shawn believed the lies that Kevyn told him about me. Consequently, he would greet me with hostility. He hated the ground that I walked on all because of my so-called best friend. Unbeknownst to me, Kevyn was sleeping with him the entire time. As usual, he dumped Shawn after he had used him. Shawn was hurt and had the nerve to call me to find out why Kevyn dissed him. That's when the truth came out.

I forgave Kevyn for that stunt. I looked over his transgression because I felt that I needed him because I was right in the middle of my sadness. I put Shawn out of my mind and never gave much thought to what Kevyn had done. If I was being evil according to Kevyn, I had every right to do so. After all the conniving things he had done to me and other people, he certainly had it coming.

My phone ranged. I picked it up after the third ring.

"Hello," I answered.

"You ain't shit bitch! You won't be happy with Milton. I'll make sure of that." Kevyn yelled into the phone.

"I'm not worried about your sorry ass Kevyn. As far as I'm concerned you don't exist."

"Fuck you! You crazy ass bitch!"

"You feel better now? Good." I said as I slammed the phone down again.

That was typical of Kevyn, trying to retaliate after he couldn't get what he wanted. I wasn't having it anymore. I was sick and tired of playing his childish game.

My phone ranged again. I was sure it was Kevyn with something else to say.

I picked it up after the first ring.

"Hello," I said in a firm tone.

"What's the matter, Dae'Mon? Afraid of me, huh? Well, you better be cuz I'm gonna fuck you up when I see you." Kevyn screamed into the phone.

"You ain't gonna do a fucking thing to me!" I said in a condescending tone.

"You'll learn not to fuck with me, bitch!"

"Ooh, You really got me scared. I'm sitting over here shaking in my boots. I'm warning you! If you put one hand on me, I promise you I'll kick your bitch ass!"

"We'll just see about that! Mothafucker!"

"Kevyn, eat me! You're just mad because you can't have your way this time. Get use to it bitch! Milton and I are together now. So fuck off!" With that said, I slammed the phone down for the third time.

What puzzled me was the fact that Kevyn was going to great extremes to keep Milton and I apart. He knew just as well as I did that I could beat the shit out of him. Did that stop him from going there? No.

My phone ranged again. I decided to put a stop to the madness. I yanked the phone off of the cradle after the first ring.

"Bitch, you call my house one more time. I promise you I will come over there and kick yo muthafucking ass!" I yelled into the receiver.

"Dae'Mon baby, who are you talking to like that?"

It was Milton. I was so happy to hear his voice.

"Baby, I'm so sorry. I thought you were Kevyn. How are you?" I said softly.

"I'm cool. What has Kevyn done?" Milton questioned.

"I don't want to talk about it."

"Well, you're gonna talk about it! I thought I told you that we would handle this together?" Milton said sternly.

"Yes, you did. I'm sorry but I was trying to amend the situation on my own."

"Dae'Mon, I'm so disappointed in you."

I felt tears welling up in my eyes. The last thing I wanted to do was to cause more friction. I needed Milton's support, not his anger.

"Milton, I'm sorry. I didn't mean to…"

"Sorry, just isn't good enough Dae'Mon!"

I felt a tear stream down my face. "Milton, please don't be angry. I was trying to do the right thing by my friend. I didn't mean any disrespect. I feel just awful."

"Well maybe next time, you will listen to me!"

"Baby, please don't yell at me. I need your support. I said as I struggled to keep my tears from flowing.

"Don't even try that crying shit with me Dae'Mon. When I tell you something, I expect for you to listen. Do I make myself clear?" Milton said sternly.

"Yes! Please don't be angry with me!" I said as I dried my eyes.

"I'm not angry with you. In the future, all I ask is that you don't disrespect my manhood. I'm crazy about you boy. Now give daddy a kiss!"

"What?"

"Give daddy a kiss," Milton said laughing.

"Ok." I said as I made a kissing noise into the phone.

"Thank you. I needed that. Well, I just want to let you know that I should be there about 2:30. Ok?"

"Yes, daddy," I said smiling.

"And you know this! Can't wait to see you! Bye my luv," Milton said.

"See you soon." I said as I hung up the phone.

I was very remorseful that Kevyn and I were still at odds. I thought we could put the whole incident behind us, but Kevyn was being difficult as usual. I wanted things to go back to the way they were before when we were friends. Well, almost the way it was just with Milton included in the equation!

CHAPTER TWELVE

I had just settled down for a quick nap when I heard the doorbell ringing. I figured it was Milton, but to my surprise Justice was standing at my front door with a gloomy look on her face. I didn't want any more drama, so I was somewhat hesitant to open the door.

I decided not to leave her standing out in the cold, so I invited her inside my loft. I could tell by the look on her face that something was on her mind. I smiled and gave her a big hug and just waited for the floodgates to open. Justice released herself from my embrace and began to speak.

"Dae'Mon, I apologize for just dropping by unannounced, but I wanted to let you know that I love you and I'm sorry for what Kevyn put you through." Justice said with sadness in her voice.

"I love you too, and you have nothing to be sorry for. This is Kevyn's doing."

"I know, but you deserve to be happy. I hate what Kevyn did."

"Justice, Milton and I are going to be together and that's something Kevyn will just have to get use to. I let him get away from me once, but I refuse to do it again."

"I don't know why you did it in the first place. Kevyn knew Milton didn't want him. He told me that several times. He said that it was just fun messing with him.

"Justice you're lying." I said as I lead her to the sofa. "Explain to me why Kevyn is being such an ass then!"

"Because he's jealous that you got what he couldn't get! Also, I never told you but he has always wanted to be like you. He has never felt that he is as good as you are."

"What do you mean?" I questioned.

"Well look at all that you have accomplished. You have a degree, a very nice job, your own place, and he works at a clothing store in Bannister Mall. He just feels inadequate around you."

"Really?" I never knew that."

"There's a lot you don't know, but we're not going to go there. Just be happy that Milton wanted you! Damn Kevyn!"

"Justice, I'm so happy that you stopped by. I thought you were mad at me."

"No, I could never be angry with you. Actually, I'm very proud of you."

"Why?"

I was depressed about the situation, but Justice's support made me feel good. It appeared to me that she felt that Kevyn was in the wrong. I didn't want to say anything negative because she could have been running a game on me. That was a chance that I wasn't willing to take, so I allowed her to take the lead.

"Well for starters, you followed your heart this time and didn't allow Kevyn to keep you from Milton. Secondly, I'm proud of you for slapping the shit out of him. Honey, he was wrecked when I walked him to his car. I'm just glad that someone finally showed him that this world is not all about him."

"Justice, I feel just awful for hitting him. I didn't mean to hurt him."

"Hurt him! Honey, get a grip! He's being hurting you for years. Dae'Mon, this may make you angry, but I'm going to tell you anyway. Kevyn purposely set out to keep you and Milton apart."

"Why do you say that?" I inquired.

"Well Kevyn never told you that he went over to Milton's house trying to get with him. Milton threw him out but not before he confessed his desire for you. Kevyn was livid. He vowed to do anything to keep you two apart."

I felt the blood rushing to my head. I was furious. I wanted to drive over to Kevyn's apartment and beat the hell out of him for what he had being doing. Milton was telling the truth about Kevyn. I was so naïve.

"That fucking bastard! I refused to believe it when the story was told to me. I've been such a fool!" I said as I laid back on the sofa.

"Don't worry about it! He got exactly what he deserved. Knocked on his ass!" Justice said laughing.

"Girl that's not funny."

"Yes it is. You should have seen the look on his face when you hit him. It was truly a Kodak moment. So yes, it's very funny. I had to contain myself from laughing when we left the party. When I got in my car though, I laughed so hard that I almost pissed on myself."

"Justice, you are a fool. It's still not right. I shouldn't have hit him."

"Yeah, yeah, yeah! Like I said before, he got exactly what he deserved. Anyway, enough about him! Now, I want the juicy details of what happened at the party between you and Milton." Justice said with a big smile on her face.

"Whatever do you mean?" I teased.

"Don't play me for crazy! I'm talking about that magical kiss I heard everyone talking about. Now, do you remember?" Justice asked with her eyebrows raised.

"What kiss? I didn't do anything."

"Umm huh! That's not what I heard. I heard that it would have taken a crowbar to pry you two apart."

We laughed.

"Who? Me?"

"Listen here, Miss Thing! I want to know about this kiss. I heard it was so hot it could melt butter." Justice said as she tilted her head to the side.

"Alright I'll tell you. Well, Milton kept going on and on about how he wanted to be with me, and he didn't understand why I continued to refuse him. I wasn't saying anything, so he grabbed me and planted a deep kiss on me."

"You go bitch!" Justice laughed.

"Girl, I tried to push him away, but it was just too good. I was just as happy as a sissy with a bag full of dicks."

Justice fell back on the sofa laughing.

"Boy, you are a fool." Justice said.

"I have never been kissed like that before. I felt like a school girl getting her first kiss."

"I'm so happy that you finally came to your senses. I never said anything, but it always puzzled me why you didn't fight harder for Milton when it was obvious how much you wanted him."

I sat straight up on the sofa and crossed my legs. I couldn't believe what I was hearing.

"Wait a minute! You mean to tell me that you felt this way and never said anything? I questioned.

"Yeah I did. I even told Kevyn that I thought you and Milton would make a good couple, but you know he wasn't trying to hear that."

"Why didn't you say anything to me?"

"Because I didn't want to get in your business."

"Girl, when are you not in somebody's business?" I said laughing.

"Whatever! I hope you don't get mad at me for saying this, but you were very bitter and angry back then." Justice said.

"Yeah, you're right. I was still not over Winton, and I have to be honest with myself and say that I would have found some way to ruin it."

"Exactly! But now you have cleared your head and are ready to make it work. I'm so excited for you. You deserve only the best that life has to offer." Justice said.

She reached over, hugged me, and gave me a quick smack on the lips. It was during these times that I treasured her friendship the most. I finally got the encouragement and support I needed to make a relationship with Milton work. I pulled away from Justice as tears slowly streamed down my face.

"Baby boy, why are you crying?" Justice questioned.

"For so many different reasons. I'm happy that Milton and I are finally together. I'm sad that Kevyn cannot share in my joy, and I'm sad because I may have lost him forever." I began to sob.

"Dae'Mon, look at me." Justice said as she pulled my face up with her hand. "You have nothing to be sad about. This is all because Kevyn is being selfish. I want you to promise me that you won't allow this to bother you? I want you to make that fine man of yours happy. Promise me!"

"I'll try my best." I whispered as I dried my eyes.

"You are truly one of the most beautiful people I know. I can always count on you keeping it real even when I don't like what you say, but deep down inside I know you're right. I have always loved your honesty and your sincerity. No one can ever say that you're not a true friend. Now hold your head up and be happy!" Justice said as a smile grew on her face.

"Yeah, I know you're right, and that's what makes it so hard knowing that I have been a good friend to Kevyn and having him turn on me like this."

I could feel the tears welling up in my eyes again. I wanted to let them flow freely, but this time something was holding them back. It was as if the first set of tears brought me out of a dark hole. I was beginning to feel better about the situation.

"Excuse my expression, but the hell with Kevyn! You have a real man in your life. He is your concern now, not that childish friend of ours. Trust me, he will come around again. No one puts up with his shit like you do, not even me."

Justice stood up and placed her purse strap over her arm. She turned to me and motioned for me to stand up. I rose to my feet and placed myself in Justice's extended arms. She gave me a long, deep hug. I felt good being in her arms, and I didn't want to let go.

"Dae'Mon, I can't breathe." Justice said gasping for air as if I was squeezing the life out of her. We laughed as we released each other from the embrace.

"I'm sorry." I said. "I'm just glad to have you as a friend. Your support means the world to me."

"Thank you. Your love and support mean the world to me also."

"It's amazing how you can be a royal bitch at times, but sweet and caring when you need to be." I said.

"I'll let you slide with that one. Besides, I have to keep that tough girl image to ward away those fools."

We laughed.

"Yeah, I understand where you're coming from. Justice, I want you to promise me that if we ever have a disagreement that we will always sit down and discuss it instead harboring resentment towards one another."

"I promise and I want you to do the same."

"I will. You have my word on that."

"I'm glad to hear that. Well, I have to get going. I have to go check on Kevyn, and I don't want to be here when your man cums over." Justice laughed.

"Very funny witch. He should be on his way as we speak. Good luck with Kevyn." I said.

"Well, let me go. Give me another hug."

Just as Justice and I embraced, there was a knock at the door. This time I was sure it was Milton. I didn't want any more surprises!

"Shit, I didn't want to be here when Milton arrived." Justice said.

"Well, he doesn't bite." I said as I walked to the door.

I looked through the peephole, and I was elated that it was Milton standing there. I opened the door. His smile seemed to fill the room. I started giggling like a silly schoolgirl. Justice walked toward the door to leave.

"Dae'Mon, let the man in before he catches a cold." Justice said laughing.

Milton walked inside my loft and extended his right hand to Justice while holding a shopping bag in the other.

"I'm Milton, it's a pleasure to meet you."

"I'm Justice and the pleasure is all mine. Well, I was on my way out, so I have to say hello and good-bye. You take care of my friend." Justice said as she headed out the door.

"You have my word. Be careful!" Milton said.

"I will. See you guys later." Justice said as she left the building.

I closed the door after Justice drove off. I was sad to see her leave, but I was excited to see Milton again. He still had a big smile on his face, and I was smiling too.

"Hi baby." I said as I planted a deep kiss on his lips.

"Wow, what a greeting!" Milton said as our lips parted.

"I missed you."

"I missed you more. Not to worry, I'm here now."

Little did I know that I was in for a big surprise...

CHAPTER THIRTEEN

Thoughtful! That was the best word to describe Milton. I was in utter shock when I found out that the items in the shopping bag were gifts for me. I was excited. What could I say? I enjoyed being pampered. I wasn't expecting to get any more gifts since Christmas had already passed.

Milton could see the excitement in my eyes, so he toyed with me. My curiosity got the better of me, and I couldn't take it anymore.

"Milton, please show me what's in the bags." I pleaded.

"Baby, you're gonna have to wait until I'm ready to give them to you." Milton said with a smile on his face.

"Oh, baby! Please…" I begged.

"Don't beg! It doesn't become you."

"Ok, I'll have my revenge later."

"Did I make the baby angry?" Milton laughed.

"I don't get angry. I get even." I retorted.

"Ok, give me your best shot!"

With that said, I grabbed Milton and passionately kissed his lips while he struggled to maintain his balance. The force of the kiss caught him by surprise. He quickly gained his balance and kissed me with just as much fervor and hunger as I had kissed him. We stopped kissing as Milton looked into my eyes.

"Is this your way of trying to seduce those gifts from me?" Milton questioned.

"Would I do something like that?" I said in my best Erkol voice.

"Yes and you know it."

"I'm ashamed you would think such a thing of little old me." I said laughing.

"Ok, I'll give them to you tomorrow then." Milton stated.

"Ok, whatever you say! You're the boss."

I was playing along, and I was going to show Milton that I was better at playing this waiting game than he was. As the saying goes, if you can't beat them, join them! Kevyn told me to always pretend as if I don't care, and I was bound to get what I wanted. Now, I had to see if this little strategy would work.

"Milton, what's on the agenda for this evening?" I asked.

"How about a little bump and grind?"

"With you?"

"Yeah, of course with me. Did you think I was talking about the Easter Bunny?"

"You're such a smartass. Well, I don't do things like that. I'm not that way."

"Yeah right! And fat meat ain't greasy."

We laughed.

"Honestly! I'm not gay. I just prefer the company of a man." I said.

"Ok for preferring the company of a man. I prefer your company."

"Oh no, Mother would never approve."

"I asked her. She said it's ok for us to play with each other." Milton countered.

"Let's us pray!"

We laughed.

"You're not going to be laughing when you don't get these gifts."

"That's your business. If that's what you want to do, then be my guest." I said.

"Oh, I know this game. Pretend as if you don't care and I will give in. You have to get up earlier than that to pull one over me."

"Obviously not! Looks as if someone beat me to it." I said.

"What does that suppose to mean?" Milton questioned.

"Nothing, I was just saying."

"I'll show you not to make jokes about me."

Milton chased me into the bedroom where I tried to hide but to no avail. Milton grabbed me from behind and began to tickle me. I was kicking and screaming like a mad man. I didn't like to be tickled, and I was trying to free myself from Milton's grasp. He was too strong, and I couldn't escape. He kept tickling me until tears began to run down my face.

Somehow, I managed to free myself from his clutches. He sat on the edge of the bed laughing at me as I laid on the floor trying to catch my breath.

"Milton, I'm gonna get you back when you least expect." I said in between breaths.

"I'm afraid. Look I'm shaking."

"Ok, buster…We'll just see about that."

"Come here baby." Milton said as he rose to his feet.

He reached to help me up from the floor. As I stood facing him, he put his arms around my waist and starred into my eyes.

"I'm not letting you off the hook that easily. You shall be punished." I said.

He laughed.

It was refreshing to have someone in my life like Milton. He had a wonderful sense of humor and wasn't uptight about life. I felt a happiness that had been missing for many years. It was just amazing how in the course of one evening, my joy was restored. Before I knew it, a smile had crept on my face.

"What are you smiling about?" Milton questioned.

"I'm smiling about you." I said.

"Me? What did I do?"

"You have made me so happy. That's all."

"Good. I'm glad I can make you happy. You make me happy too." He said.

We kissed as Milton began to massage my back. I became aroused from his touch, so I shifted my weight to conceal my excitement. Our lips parted after an intense kissing session. Milton exited the room and headed to the bathroom. I stood motionless until I heard water running in the bathroom. I ran into the living room searching for the shopping bags. I couldn't find them. I wondered to myself where Milton had hidden them. I tiptoed back to the bedroom so Milton wouldn't find out what I was up to. As soon as I laid down on the bed, the water stopped running. Milton appeared in front of the bedroom door with a huge smile on his face.

"Baby, what are you up to?" I inquired.

"Nothing." Milton said in a childlike voice.

"Doesn't seem that way to me!" I replied.

"Dae'Mon, come here." Milton said.

I was somewhat suspicious. Milton was acting very peculiar. I knew he was up to something, but I couldn't quite figure out what it was until he opened the door to the bathroom. It was astonishing! There were rose petals on the floor and in the tub. He had scented candles strategically placed in every corner of the room. My mouth dropped, and I was at a lost for words.

Milton grabbed me by the hand and led me into the bathroom. I stood motionless as he began to undress me. He led me to the tub and motioned for me to get in the water. I felt as if I was floating on cloud 9. I settled into the tub to begin my bath. I was surprised that Milton used milk instead of regular bubble bath. I didn't mind cuz I had never had one before.

"Baby, this is so sweet." I said.

"Anything for my sweetheart. Wait, I'll be right back." Milton said as he exited the bathroom.

I didn't think it could get any better than it already was, but I was mistaken. I suddenly heard Maxwell's voice bellowing through my loft. I was really feeling it. Milton walked back into the bathroom with two glasses of what appeared to be White Zinfandel. I squealed with delight as

Milton handed me the glass. I took a sip and laid back in the tub enjoying the moment.

Milton began to rub my body slightly with the rose petals. I became aroused and tried to pull him into the tub with me.

"No, this is for you." He said.

"Baby, please join me."

"No, this is your moment." He said as he continued to rub my body with the petals.

I took another sip of the wine and rested against the back of the tub with my eyes closed. I was overjoyed with my special treatment. No one had ever done anything so nice for me. I became so overcome with emotion that tears slowly rolled down my face. Milton noticed and suddenly stopped caressing me.

"Baby, what's the matter?" he questioned.

"I'm just happy. No one has ever been so attentive to me." I whimpered.

"Baby, there's much more than this to come." Milton said as he wiped the tears from my eyes.

"You are too good to me, Milton. I don't know how I can ever thank you."

"Just love me baby! That's all I ask of you." Milton said with a smile.

I stood up in the tub and motioned for Milton to stand up. I hugged him as if he was the last man on earth. I began to kiss his lips, getting his clothes wet. We laughed as our lips parted. Milton took my nude body into his arms and began to slowly remove the water from it with a warm towel. I was in ecstasy.

After I was dry, Milton put my robe around my shoulders and carried me to the bedroom. I wrapped my arms around his neck and nibbled on his ear. He giggled like a child with every lick. As we entered the room, I smiled upon seeing two boxes situated on the feather down pillows on my bed. I quickly jumped out of Milton's arms and ran over to the gifts. I tore into the first box with the precision of a Gingsu Knife. To my surprise, it was a bottle of Contradiction for men. I had planned to buy a bottle after I got a sample at Bannister Mall while I was out Christmas shopping. Milton must have had ESP.

"Oh Milton, how did you know I wanted this cologne?" I asked.

"Lucky guess!" He said smiling.

We kissed.

I tore into the second box and yelped like a dog in heat. Hey, I got excited when I saw what was inside of the package. It was pair of Leopard print silk boxers.

"Baby, you are too good to me. Thank you!" I said crying.

"You're welcome. Anything for my love." Milton said as he wiped my eyes.

It was an emotional time for me. It had been a long time since someone had treated me like royalty. I was grateful for Milton's thoughtfulness, and I was excited about the new love of my life.

I would soon discover that Milton was full of surprises.

CHAPTER FOURTEEN

Later that evening, I laid in bed basking in heavenly bliss. Milton's surprise made me feel like a million and one dollars. My emotions were running wild. My hormones were surging. I was surprised I didn't go up in flames from my exhilaration.

The sound of a car alarm brought my thoughts to a screeching halt. The alarm sounded like the one I had installed in my 1999 Honda Prelude. I got out of bed to investigate.

As I looked out of the window, I could see the lights on my car flashing. There were little shiny objects lying on the ground next to the car. I didn't know what they were or how they got there. I threw on a pair of sweats to go take a look.

"Dae'Mon, where are you going?" Milton questioned.

"I'm going outside to check on my car. My alarm is going off. I'll be right back."

"Ok."

As I opened the front door of the building, I could see glass around my car. I walked around to the street to get a closer look. To my horror, a brick had been thrown though the drivers side window. I immediately ran back to my loft.

"Milton, someone through a brick through my window. I bet you it was that muthafucking Kevyn."

"What! Did you see him?" Milton asked.

"No, but I have been living here three years and nothing like this has ever happened. Now, I get a brick through my window. I'm gonna fuck him up." I said as I wandered around aimlessly.

"Dae'Mon, calm down. You don't know for sure if it was him."

"Well, he's the only one mad enough at me to do something like that. I'm kicking his ass. Fucking bitch!" I screamed.

"Dae'Mon, calm the fuck down!" Milton yelled as he grabbed my arm. "I want you to call the police so they can take a report. Someone could have seen whoever did this."

"I'm not calling the fucking police because I already know who did it. It's gonna take the police to pull me off of his ass." I said as I pulled away from Milton.

I was headed to Kevyn's apartment to give him a beat down, Southern Style. Milton gazed at me like a hawk as I scurried around my bedroom looking for my gym shoes.

"Dae'Mon, you sit your got-damn ass down right now!" Milton screamed.

"Milton…"

"I don't want to hear it! Now sit down!" Milton demanded.

I took a seat on the edge of the bed. I was fuming, and Milton was holding up the progress of me beating the hell out of Kevyn.

"Dae'Mon, I'm really disappointed with you. You're very irrational and acting immature. What are you going to accomplish by fighting Kevyn? What will happen is your little smart-ass will be put in jail for assault. Then what?"

"But Milton, he damaged my car." I whined.

"I don't care! You need to handle this situation the right way. You could be hurt or even worse, killed. All over something that you don't have any proof that Kevyn did."

"But I know he did. I just feel it."

I stood up and began to pace back and forth. I wanted revenge. I wasn't trying to hear that legal stuff that Milton was talking about. I thought about stealing on him just so I could leave to handle my business.

"Whatever happened to innocent until proven guilty? Dae'Mon, you really need to call the police and let them handle this."

"No, the best thing for me to do is put my foot in his…"

"I'm getting very annoyed with you right now. I'm warning you. If I hear that you have been involved in a fight with Kevyn, then I'm whopping your ass. Understood?" Milton stated in a matter of fact tone.

"Well, I guess you're just gonna have to whop my ass then because I'm gonna get him."

If looks could kill...

"You take your little ignorant ass over there then. I hope Kevyn beats the hell out of you and then send your dumb ass to jail." Milton said as he walked out of the room.

"But Milton..."

"Don't fucking call me when they lock your ass up!" Milton yelled from the hall.

I walked into the living room to find Milton stretched out on the sofa. I went over to him.

"Milton, I'm sorry."

"Don't fucking touch me!" Milton said as he jerked his arm away from me.

"Please don't' be angry with me. I'm just upset." I countered.

"That doesn't give you the right to act like an ass. Leave me alone!"

I walked away wounded with tears streaming down my face. Milton was absolutely right. I was being immature. I was hurt that Kevyn's anger was taken out on my car instead of me. I wanted to hurt him, so he could know how I felt. I decided that it would be in my best interest to call the police as instructed.

I dialed 911. An operator came on the line. I gave her my information. I was told that an officer would be dispatched to my address. She failed to inform me that it would take two hours for someone to arrive.

Milton was still not speaking to me. He stayed in the living room away from me. I laid across the bed staring into space, and then I heard a knock at the door. I figured it was the police.

"Dae'Mon, the police are here to see you." Milton yelled from the living room.

I quickly put on my clothes and headed to the living room. The two uniformed officers were standing in front of the door.

"I'm Dae'Mon Greene."

"I'm Officer Jones and this is Officer Wilson. We received a call about a vandalized car." He said as he walked over to me and extended his hand.

We shook hands. Officer Jones was very attractive. I pinched myself for being attracted to him with Milton in the same room.

"Yes, a brick was thrown through my window on the drivers side."

"Did you get a look at the person?" Officer Wilson asked.

"No sir, I was in my bedroom when I heard the car alarm go off."

"Do you have any idea who would want to do something like this to you?" Officer Jones questioned.

Milton gave me a not so pleasing look. I looked away feeling that again it would be in my best interest for my answer to begin with the letter N.

"No sir."

"Ok, Mr. Greene. We will take pictures of the car to place in the file. We'll talk to your neighbors to see if anyone saw anything. Here's my card if you any questions or additional information."

I took the card from Officer Jones' hand. I could feel his eyes undressing me. I studied the blue writing on the card. I was trying to keep my mind free and not fantasize about Officer Jones all the while wanting to tell him that I thought my friend Kevyn had damaged my car, but I knew I wouldn't hear the end of it from Milton.

"Thank you sir. Please keep me posted!" I stated.

"Will do Mr. Greene." Officer Jones said as he shook my hand again with a seductive smile on his face.

I quickly glanced away as I opened the door for them to leave. I closed the door behind them as they walked into the hall. I turned to go back to the bedroom. Milton grabbed my arm. I began to shake. I didn't know what to expect from him. I stood still.

"Dae'Mon, I want to apologize for yelling at you earlier. I just wanted you to understand the consequences of your actions if you assaulted Kevyn. I'm proud of you for doing the right thing in calling the police. I don't want you to be angry with me."

I wrapped my arms around his neck as he wrapped his muscular arms around my waist. I held him tightly inhaling his scent. He smelt good. My anger began to short circuit.

"Sweetheart, I'm not angry with you. I'm just glad you are able to overlook my childish behavior."

We separated from our embrace. We held hands as we stared into each other's eyes. We stood in silence for which seemed like an eternity. Milton finally broke the silence.

"Let's go to bed, Sweetie"

"Ok, that sounds good to me."

Milton and I walked to the bedroom hand and hand. We smiled at each other along the way. We crawled into bed and pulled the covers over us.

CHAPTER FIFTEEN

Milton carried me to the bedroom. He grabbed my wrists and pinned me down on the bed. He began to ferociously kiss my lips with the intensity of a violent thunderstorm. His mouth hungered for the sweet taste of my juicy lips and I for his. He separated his lips from my mouth only to tease my neck with his tongue. He slowly removed my robe as he continued to devour me. I laid in my nakedness moaning softly.

His hands shook as he gently massaged my chest, tracing every curve and patch of hair. He lowered his head to my chest, licking and tasting it. I could feel my body heat rising to a boil. He clasped his lips around my nipple, pulling it into his mouth as he began to suck it with such a force that caused me to cry out in pleasure. He shifted to the other nipple, surrounding it with his lips. Tiny eruptions of pleasure exploded in my body. I was about to climax, but I resisted. I wanted to enjoy the moment for a while longer.

He dragged his way back to my lips. We kissed with such passion that our moaning became louder in volume. Our legs intertwined as he massaged my thighs. I massaged his juicy ass as he slowly thrust up and down. I became frantic. Milton scrambled to a sitting position. His erection pointed at me as I caressed it between my fingers. He was losing control. He parted my legs and gently massaged my love-canal. He looked at me with lust in his eyes. I knew what he wanted. I wanted it too. I hungered to feel him inside of me. He slowly pushed my legs toward my torso. I arched my back to offer him the prize. He slowly slid inside. It was magical.

He thrust all the way in. My breath was trapped in my throat. I couldn't say a word. The sensation was so great I couldn't bear it. I began to dig my nails into his back as his erection penetrated my opening. I wanted more. I wrapped my legs around his waist and met him stroke for stroke as he began to thrust back and forth. He groaned and began to thrust faster and deeper. I screamed out in pure delight. I could feel the fire of his body transferring to mine.

He stared down at me, his gaze were like laser beams burning deep inside my soul. I slid my hands down his back onto his moving ass. I palmed his melons pushing him deeper, harder and faster inside of me. I wanted his body to melt into mine.

I could tell he was getting close to climaxing after he buried his face into crevice of my neck. He was fighting hard to continue the motion, but was losing the battle each passing second. I didn't want him to stop. I wanted to continue for as long as we could stand it.

I felt the intensity building up in my body. My muscles grew tighter and tighter around his love tool. His face became distorted like something out of a horror movie. The time was fast approaching. We were peaking at the same time. He screamed out my name.

"Dae'Mon, you feel so good."

My breath had abandoned me again. I was trying to hold on for the last stretch, but I was fighting to no avail. My muscles became even tighter around his erection as he screamed out in pleasure. I felt his body tightening and converging, just waiting to free the fruit of our lovemaking. We both had reached the moment of truth. I clung to him waiting for our pleasure to spin itself out. It was about to happen.

"Dae'Mon, I can't hold it any longer." Milton cried out.

"Let it go baby, let it go!" I responded with just as much fire.

"Ok, I'm…

Ring…Ring…Ring…

Noooo! Can you believe that? I was in ecstasy. Then the damn phone ranged. I was awakened from my pleasurable dream. The wet spot in my underwear was a clear sign that I was enjoying myself just a tad too much.

I yanked the phone from the cradle. I wanted revenge for this intrusion.

"Hello!" I snapped.

"Dae'Mon, how are you?" the voice questioned.

"I'm fine. Who is this?" I said in a nasty tone.

"Fool, it's Caleb. Happy New Year."

"Oh my God! Caleb, how are you? And Happy New Year to you."

Caleb Dinard Wright had been one of my best friends since we met in college 7 years ago at the University of Kansas. He resided in Tucson, Arizona and was an associate professor of business at UofA. That's the University of Arizona for those of you who didn't know. I hadn't seen Caleb since '96 when he came to visit for my 26th birthday.

"You must be getting some dick with the way you answered that phone." Caleb said laughing.

"Very funny, witch. No, my man is laying beside me right now."

"What! You got a man? I don't believe it!"

"What does that suppose to mean? You act as if I'm not capable of getting a man?" I countered.

Caleb was right. It had been a long time since I had a man. He knew that I wasn't entertaining the idea of being with someone, so I could understand why it was such a shock to him. However, he didn't have to make it sound as if I had smallpox or something.

"Well, you know how you are! You have been running from love ever since that fool, Winton, ran out on you. I'm glad you have finally gotten over that ordeal. Now, dish the dirt. Who is he?" Caleb questioned.

"You remember Milton Parker don't you? The guy I pointed out to you in '96 at Connections."

"Bitch, get out of town! That fine man! You are so lucky. I told you to snatch that man up, but you wouldn't.

I'm glad that you finally came to your senses. Otherwise, I was gonna get me a piece of that." Caleb laughed.

"Well, we don't have to worry about that now. I got him and he's not going anywhere."

"I ain't mad at ya! Wait a minute! Didn't you tell me that you were not going to get with Milton because of that silly fool Kevyn? How did you pull this one off?" Caleb questioned.

"Well, he's mad at me because he walked up when Milton and I were kissing. He went off on me and cussed me out in front of everyone at the party. I was so embarrassed. I smacked the hell out of him before I knew it, and now someone has broken the driver's side window on my car."

"Probably that stupid bitch, Kevyn! I hope you called the police."

"Yes I did. I don't have any proof it was him, so I just filed a report. I'll find out who did. It's bound to come to the light one way or the other."

"Yeah, you're probably right. Don't worry about it. If something else happens, you just call me; and I'll be there in a heartbeat."

"Thanks for your support, it means the world to me. I really feel bad though for smacking Kevyn."

"Well you shouldn't! It's about time that stupid little twit got what he deserved. I wish you had whopped his ass instead. I will never understand why you befriended someone so shallow. Milton kissed you? Oooh!" Caleb said quickly changing the subject.

Caleb had a strong dislike for Kevyn. They got into a huge argument during Caleb's visit. Kevyn was mad because someone else was taking my attention away from him. He was very rude and nasty to Caleb. Caleb being the professional by day and a bitch by night didn't go for that. He read Kevyn up one side and down the other. They would have come to blows had Justice and I not separated them.

Caleb felt that all Kevyn needed was a good ass beating and he would learn some respect. How true!

I was so into my conversation with Caleb that I hadn't noticed that Milton had sat up on the bed watching me. He was looking so cute and had the biggest smile on his face. I wanted to jump on him and have my way.

"Yes, Milton kissed me without warning in front of all those people. How can I ever live this down?" I stated.

"Please! You enjoyed that kiss just as much as you enjoyed it being from Milton. Don't forget who you're talking to! I know you like a book. And I bet you Milton has already rocked your world?" Caleb said laughing.

"I never said I didn't enjoy the kiss. It was just I didn't expect it since I had been running for him for so long. I guess he got tired of waiting." I said as I rubbed Milton's leg.

Milton smiled and kissed me on the lips. I felt sparks. I was thinking about that dream I had. I wanted to put the phone down and recreate my fantasy. Caleb must have been reading my mind.

"Well, I just heard a smacking sound, so I'll take that as my queue to call you later. I want all of the details because I know he done hit it." Caleb said.

"You need to stop. Ok, I will call you later. Happy New Year and I will chat with you real soon."

"Ok bye now and tell him to treat my sister right."

We laughed.

"I will most definitely tell him what you said. Take care and don't do anything I wouldn't do." I said.

"That ain't much, bitch! Bye." Caleb said as he quickly hung up the phone.

I placed the phone back on the cradle and laughed. Caleb always brought a smile to my face. People were always surprised when he told them that he was a college professor. He just had a wonderful sense humor that could bring life to any party.

Milton was staring at me. I looked into his beautiful brown eyes and began to caress his face. He massaged my hand as he kissed it.

"Baby, what were you dreaming about earlier?" Milton asked.

How did Milton know about my dream? Was I talking in my sleep? I felt the shadow of embarrassment invading my body. I became hot all over. I looked away and didn't answer him. He put his hand on my chin and turned my face to his.

"What? Cat got your tongue?" He said.

"No, what are you talking about?" I said, playing dumb.

"You always do that! You know what I'm talking about! Oh Milton, Oh Milton! You grabbed me rubbing on me like you were a sex-crazed fool. I thought you were losing your mind. So, I guess I was wearing it out, huh?" Milton said with a big smile on his face.

"Whatever!" I said.

"Why won't you tell me what you were dreaming about?"

"It's my secret and my dream." I said.

"All I know is, I must have really been putting a number on that ass with the way you were carrying on."

Milton fell over in the bed laughing. I couldn't believe I was acting that way. Well, it was believable. The sex was incredible.

"Well, you got me. I admit that you were wearing me out. I have never had it like that before. But I can't tell you how it ended because I was awakened by the ringing of the phone." I smiled.

"I knew it. You want me to tap that ass don't you?" Milton asked seductively.

"Who's to say? Maybe I do and maybe I don't!" I shot back.

He pulled me over to him and our lips met. The sparks began to generate through my body. I could feel his body heat. We were coming alive. I don't have to get into what happened next. All I have to say is, the dream came true.

CHAPTER SIXTEEN

Let's Make A Love Scene. Joe couldn't have been more right when he made that song. Milton and I made a love scene four more times that day and three more times the following day. I was overheated, baby. Once Milton broke the seal on my can of biscuits, I couldn't get enough. I wore him out. We would rest only to get up and go at it again. We were so tired that we stayed in bed the rest of the weekend, only getting up to eat and go to the bathroom.

I was concerned about it having been five years since someone made love to me. Well, it was somewhat uncomfortable in the beginning; but after I got use to the sensation I was receiving, it became very enjoyable. I was in ecstasy. I had never done it that many times in one day.

Milton had a way of making me feel so good, and I wanted to share everything I had with him. I didn't have to tell him what to do. It was if he was already programmed on how to please me.

Until Milton came along, I never knew the true meaning of lovemaking. Sex was not enjoyable to me. There were times when I felt that I could have had a V8. I never felt special, probably because Edwin and Winton were so mechanical. They were out to get theirs and never concerned themselves with trying to satisfy me.

Milton was different though. He was so tender and passionate with me. He was more concerned with me being pleased than he was with himself. It showed each time he touched me.

I would learn over time that no matter what true love never fails.

CHAPTER SEVENTEEN

The holidays were over, and business had returned to normal. I took my car to the Honda Dealership to have the window replaced. I was still angry, but Milton did an excellent job of making me feel better.

I was embarrassed driving on the interstate with a plastic bag taped to my door to cover the hole left by the broken window. However, I didn't' have a choice. Jack Honda was located in Overland Park, Kansas about 20 miles from where I lived. I first learned about Overland Park located in Johnson County when I was in college. The place was known for its' upper middle class neighborhoods and money.

KU had a reputation of being Snob Hill because of the rich kids who attended the university from Johnson County, but I digress.

When I arrived at the dealership, the mechanic informed me that it would take two days before my car would be finished. I was offered a courtesy car, which Milton quickly declined.

"You can drive my car." Milton said as he pulled me to the side.

I laughed knowing that was Milton's way of saying that he wanted to spend more time with me. I didn't mind because I enjoyed his company. My problem was driving his 5 Series BMW. What if something happened?

"It's insured Dae'Mon, so you don't have to worry." Milton said as if he was reading my mind.

"Ok."

"It's settled. You can drop me off at work and I can get a ride from Becky. She lives across the street from me."

"No, I'll just pick you up, and you can take me home. Or better yet! How about you spending the two days with me?"

"Yeah, I can do that. I can run by the condo and get some stuff during lunch."

"Good. I'm so excited." I said as I walked back to the shop counter. "Ok, Henry I'll be back on Wednesday to get the car. If you have any problems, please give me a call."

"I certainly will, Mr. Greene."

With that said, Milton and I left the dealership. He zipped on I-35 headed back to the city. I laid the seat back trying to relax before I went to the office, something I was not looking forward to doing.

We rode in silence taking in the scene and vibing to the sounds of the breakfast gang on Hot 103 Jamz. Their antics always brought a smile to my face. Milton however had a sad look on his face as we pulled in front of his office building. I raised the seat upright.

"Milton, are you ok?" I asked.

"Yeah, I'm fine. I just can't wait to see you this evening."

"Oh you're so sweet. We have the rest of our lives together, so don't worry."

"I'm glad to hear that. I would kiss you, but I don't want to alarm anyone." Milton said as he grabbed his briefcase and got out of the car.

"Good! I'll kiss you later this evening. What time shall I pick you up?" I said as I slid over to the driver's side.

"Around 6. Here's my business card with my cell phone number on the back if you need to get in touch with me."

"Ok, here's my business card with my cell number on the back. Here's my direct line number, so you won't have to go through my assistant. You have a good day Sweetie." I said with a smile as I headed to the office.

I turned onto Main Street heading to IST. I wanted so desperately to keeping driving pass the office and go home; but it was best for me to go in since I had been out of the office since Christmas.

I decided to do as I normally did while at work, fake it. I was very good at smiling and saying, "I'm so happy to see you today." When in actuality, I wanted to say, "Get the hell out of my face!"

Don't get me wrong! My job was enjoyable at times. It was the added stuff that came with it that got on my nerves such as the whiney customers and the associates always complaining about something. I didn't care what anyone said, the customers were not always right. They were right or left-handed as Big Mama use to say. Then, the associates would come to my office snitching on each other. I was always up on the latest scandals in the office.

I had been working for IST- one of the largest mutual fund companies in the city- for five and half years. I was tired of the office politics. I was the only manager there who had a college degree, but that didn't stop them from thinking that I didn't know much. I was also the only African-American in management, which didn't help matters. I was always second-guessed and questioned about every decision I made. My department ranked number one in customer satisfaction for three years in a row, but they were still determined to make me feel inferior.

Their little ploy to keep me down didn't work. They failed to realize that I was arrogant and was not going to take a back seat to anyone. I waited until the busy season and applied for a management position with Sprint. When word got out, I was called into Mr. Preston's, our vice president, office almost everyday to make sure I was content with my job. Big Mama always told me to never show my cards. I would just smile and say, "Things couldn't be better." I knew I was lying, but I didn't want them to try to get over on me.

Sprint offered me an impressive package in Atlanta to become a vice president of their communication center. I told them I would get back to them after the New Year. I was torn between my decision of moving to Atlanta and leaving Kansas City. Then, to further complicate matters, I had just met Milton. He was a reason for me to stay. I was hoping and praying that I didn't make the wrong decision in not taking the job. Only time would tell!

The moment of truth had arrived. I pulled into IST's parking garage and just sat in the car. I didn't want to enter the building, but I knew I had to do so. As soon as I turned the corner heading to my office, I could see my secretary; I'm sorry, Executive Assistant, as she would politely correct me- smiling at me.

"Good morning, Mr. Greene. Welcome back!"

"Good morning Agnes. How are you?" I said.

"I'm just fine. How were your holidays?"

"Just fine. How were yours?" I asked as if I was interested.

Agnes was a sweet woman, but she could work my nerves like no one else. She had a squeaky voice that made her sound like Minnie Mouse and a weird sense of humor to go along with that annoying voice. She would overuse the word hon. There was a time when I thought my first name was hon. No matter what, it was always- Ok hon. I'll get right on that hon., Yes hon...uhhhh! I was so mad one day that I wanted haul off and bitch slap her, but I didn't. I got a good laugh just thinking about it though.

Agnes told me of all the wonderful gifts she received for Christmas and gave me an update on her family- the Brady Bunch in Kansas City. I listened to her just smiling wishing I were in my office. Agnes could be very long winded at times, so I had to find a way to get away from her.

"Agnes, I would love to stand here and listen, but I know I have a lot of work to do. I'll talk to you later. Ok?" I said as I headed toward my office.

"Ok, Mr. Greene. I'm so happy that you're back." Agnes yelled from her desk.

I walked into my office and just as I expected, blinking light on my voice mail, in-basket over flowing with mail. I was afraid to turn on my computer. The e-mails may jump out and grab me.

As soon as I sat down at my desk, the phone began to ring.

"IST, Dae'Mon Greene speaking." I replied.

"Hey baby, this is Milton."

"Hey darling. It's good to hear from you."

"You miss me already?" Milton teased.

"No, I have too much work to do to miss you." I laughed.

"Yeah right! You're probably fantasizing about me right now."

We laughed.

"You caught me. Let me put my clothes back on."

"Very funny! Listen, I'm calling to let you know that I have to go St. Louis to prepare for an upcoming trial." Milton stated.

"Really? You just got back to work. How long will you be gone?" I questioned.

"Until Wednesday morning." Milton replied.

"Ok, How are you getting to the airport?"

"The company is hiring a charter service."

I was amazed at how the sound of Milton's voice could brighten my spirit. I did not want him to go out of town, but I knew business came before pleasure.

"I'm gonna be lonely without you."

"Oh baby, I'll return before you know it. Then, we can spend some quality time together. I'm gonna take you out to dinner and spoil you rotten when I get back." Milton said.

"I can't wait. I promise I'll take good care of the car."

"I'm not worried about that. I don't mind my wife driving the car while I'm out of town." Milton said laughing.

91

"You have a safe trip, and I'm spanking your butt when you get back for that comment."

"I like the sound of that. I miss you"

"I miss you too my luv. I'll see you on Wednesday."

"Ok, I'll call you from the hotel." Milton stated.

"That's cool. I can't wait to hear from you."

"Ciao my luv." Milton said as he hung up the phone.

I didn't know what I was going to do with my time now that Milton was going to be out of town for two days. Well, it wasn't like I lead an interesting life before Milton came along.

I didn't want to think anymore about him being away from me, so I began to dig into the work on my desk. I cleared my voicemail, separated the letters in my in-basket, and responded to or deleted all 720 e-mails I received.

The day went by quickly. I looked at the clock and it was 4:30. The strange thing was the fact that I didn't remember taking lunch or talking to anyone. I was losing it. My concentration was suddenly broken when the phone beeped. It was Agnes.

"Mr. Greene, I have a Mr. Davis on line for you."

"Ok, send it through." I said without thinking. "This is Dae'Mon Greene. How may I help you?"

"Hi Dae'Mon, this is Jamal." The voice responded.

"Yes Jamal. How can I help you today?"

"You don't remember me do you?" he questioned.

"I'm sorry but I don't."

I was beginning to wonder if someone was playing a joke on me. I was getting angry because I had too much work to do to play on the phone.

"This is Jamal Davis, the bartender from the New Year's Party." He said.

"Hey Jamal. I'm so sorry I didn't recognize your name."

"That's cool. I figured you wouldn't remember after the night you had."

"What does that suppose to mean?" I questioned.

"Well, I heard about your little episode on the dance floor with your friend Kevyn."

"Oh my God, I'm so embarrassed. That's an ordeal that I'm trying to forget."

"I know and I know about you and Milton." Jamal stated.

"Ok, so what can I do for you?" I asked.

I became curious about the nature of the phone call especially since he knew that Milton and I were an item. I rubbed the top of my head trying to relieve the pressure I was feeling.

"Well, I still want to be your friend. I just moved here two weeks ago, and I need someone to show me around." He replied.

"Just as long as you know it's strictly a friendship. I don't want to mislead you."

"I'm a big boy. I can take it that Milton stole you away." He laughed.

"Very funny. I'm curious about something." I stated.

"What's that?"

"How did you get my work number?" I questioned.

I was anxious to hear what he had to say. I didn't remember writing my work number on the napkin that I had given him.

"Well I asked around. I was informed that you worked for IST, so I called and they found you."

"Ok, I understand."

"Dae'Mon, can we still have lunch or dinner. You promised me remember."

"Yes I did, but that's when the stakes were different."

"How so?"

"I was single." I said.

"Fair. But its just dinner between friends.

93

I didn't see any harm in meeting Jamal for lunch or dinner. Besides, Milton was out of town and it would give me something to do.

"Yeah, that's true. Ok Milton is out of town until Wednesday, so it will have to be tomorrow. I need to go home and rest after the day I have had today." I said.

"Ok, how about dinner at 7 p.m.?" Jamal asked.

"Ok, that sounds like a game plan."

"I will call you tomorrow to finalize everything."

"Ok, I look forward to hearing from you. Take care until next time."

"Have a good day Dae'Mon. I'll chat with you tomorrow." Jamal said as he hung up the phone.

I didn't think anymore about Jamal after our conversation. I went back to the work at hand. I got everything cleaned up by six and decided to head home. I needed to relax and take my mind off my job.

I arrived home and that's when the date with Jamal hit me. What had I done? Milton would kill me if he found out. I didn't want to ruin my relationship with him before it got off the ground. I wanted to cancel the dinner. Then, I thought to myself, what damage could be caused from two friends eating?

I would soon find out...

CHAPTER EIGHTEEN

I tried everything in my power to get in touch with Jamal to cancel our dinner plans but to no avail. After several failed attempts, I figured that Jamal wasn't responding to my messages because he knew I was gonna cancel on him. I couldn't blame the guy for liking me so much. He did think I was hot. Don't hate!

The time was fast approaching, and I was feeling sick. All I could think about was what Milton would do to me if he found out. I wanted to go, but I was afraid of Milton. I knew he was out of town and probably wouldn't find out, but I became paranoid because someone might see Jamal and me out and tell Milton. You know the kids could be vicious when they wanted to be.

I decided to call Caleb to see what he thought about the idea of me going out with Jamal. I could always count on him keeping it real with me. I picked up the phone and dialed Caleb's number. He picked up on the first ring.

"Hello." Caleb said.

"Hey Caleb. You must have thought I was trade for you to pick up on the first ring." I joked.

"Kiss my ass. You know I'm not waiting for a damn man. I'm an independent woman."

We laughed.

"You're trying to get some dick aren't you?" I questioned.

"Child no! I just had some last night, so I don't need anymore." Caleb responded.

I began to pace back and forth just waiting for the appropriate moment to ask Caleb about the dinner plans.

"Caleb you are a fool."

"Yeah, not as much as you. But what gives? Why aren't you with your man?" Caleb asked.

"Because he's out of town on business and won't be back until Wednesday."

"Oh, ok. So what's wrong? I can tell that something is on your mind." Caleb quizzed.

I took a seat on the sofa and started my story. If I was a smoker, I'm sure I would have lit a cigarette. I was nervous and could feel water running down my back.

"Caleb, I met this guy named Jamal at the party the night Milton and I got together. I promised to let him take me to dinner. He called me on yesterday wanting me to go, and I said yes because he knows about Milton and me. He said he only wanted to be friends. Do you think I should go?"

"Child, get a grip. You sound like a nervous wreck. It's not a big deal Dae'Mon. The guy just wants to have dinner. If he starts some shit, you can always leave. So I say you should go." Caleb responded.

"But what about Milton?" I questioned.

"Dae'Mon, pull yourself together. It's not like you're going to sleep with the man. Are you?"

"Hell no!"

"Well, what's the problem? You need to have friends outside of Milton. God knows you need better friends than that bitch Kevyn. Does he seem like a nice guy?"

"Yes, from what I can tell. He said that he is new in town and wants to make quality friends."

"Well there's your answer. Go and have fun and if Milton is all that you say he is, then there shouldn't be any problems. Ok?" Caleb stated.

You're right Caleb. Thanks for being the best friend a fag could have. I will call you when I get back to give you all the details about the party."

"You better. And Dae'Mon, have a good time. Lord knows you need it."

"I promise. I love you."

"I love you too. Have a good evening."

I placed the phone back on the cradle. I proceeded to get dress to meet Jamal for a quick bite to eat. Like clockwork, he called on time- 7:00 p.m.

"Hello." I said.

"Hello Dae'Mon. This is Jamal. How are you?"

"I'm just fine."

"Are you ready? Or have you changed your mind?" Jamal questioned.

"No, I'm ready. I was just waiting for you to call."

Jamal seemed to sense my apprehension.

"Dae'Mon, are you ok?" He questioned.

"Yeah, I'm fine. Honest!" I lied.

"Dae'Mon, I know you're probably worried about Milton finding out, but I can assure you that I have the best intentions. I don't want to come between you two. If I were in his shoes I wouldn't want anyone to come between my friend and me either. I just want to go out and have a good time as friends. You seem like a very cool person."

I still wasn't sure if I was making the right decision. I had met guys before who claimed that they only wanted to be friends only for them to put the moves on me later. I didn't want to go through that again. I had a feeling that Jamal was different, but I couldn't be too sure.

"Jamal, I understand what you're saying. I'm cool, ok? So, where are we going?" I asked.

"What type of food do you like?"

"It doesn't matter. I'm sure I can find something to eat no matter where we go."

"Ok, then do you want to meet me somewhere or should I come and get you?"

"You can come and get me."

The words flew out of my mouth before I knew it, and it was too late for me to take them back. Besides, I didn't want to take Milton's car.

"Ok, I need directions."

I gave Jamal directions to my loft. I must have been out of my mind because he could show up at my place anytime without calling. Milton would have my ass for sure if Jamal showed up unannounced for that fact, if he showed up at all.

Jamal picked me up and took me to the Cheesecake Factory on the Plaza. I thought it was strange for us to go to such an expensive restaurant. I tried not to feed too much into it just so I could eat in peace. I was paranoid enough as it was, so I tried to relax and enjoy myself.

Jamal and I were sitting at the table enjoying our meals when out of nowhere came David Kelly and his entourage. David Kelly was one of the messiest people in Kansas City. Every time something went down, you could be assured that David Kelly was behind it. I knew he was coming to our table as soon as he saw me.

I panicked as I saw him approaching us. Jamal had a look of concern on his face. He grabbed my arm as he spoke.

"Dae'Mon, what's wrong?"

"David Kelly the troublemaker is on his way over. I know word is going to get back to Milton now." I said in an exasperated tone.

"Dae'Mon, I told you not to worry. We're just having dinner." Jamal replied.

"Yeah that's easy for you to say. You're not dating Milton Parker."

Before Jamal could respond. David walked up to the table as if we were old friends. He knew I didn't like him. We almost came to blows one night at Connections. I knew the only reason he came over was to get some dirt.

"Hello ladies. How are we this evening?" David said.

"What do you want David?" I snapped.

David took a seat at the table. I was furious. How dare he invade my personal space?

"Dae'Mon, why are you so hostile? I just came over to say hello."

"Hello and goodbye. Poof, be gone!" I said with my hand extended outright.

"Where is all this attitude coming from?"

"Bitch, don't patronize me! Please just leave us the hell alone!" I said in angry whisper.

"Dae'Mon, I'm sure Milton wouldn't approve of you behaving this way."

Yes, he went there. I guess he thought he was calling me out or something. He wasn't aware of the fact that Jamal already knew about Milton. That only added more fuel to my fire, and I was about to explode on his ass.

"What! Let me tell you something you little trifling bitch! I will fuck you up." I said as I jumped up from the table. Jamal grabbed my arm.

People were staring at us, but I didn't care. I wanted to send David a clear message that I wasn't having it.

"Dae'Mon, no!" Jamal screamed.

"No, Jamal let me go! I'm gonna teach this bitch a lesson once and for all. I'm tired of this."

The staff at the restaurant ran over to our table and escorted David away from me. I saw red and wanted to kick his ass right where we stood. Jamal was trying to calm me down, but I wasn't hearing it. I could hear David screaming from the front of the restaurant.

"You won't be as happy when Milton finds out, bitch!"

That did it! I went to get up from my chair, but Jamal gripped my arm tightly so I couldn't leave. He knew what I was about to do.

"Dae'Mon, that trash is not worth it. Forget about him and finish your meal." Jamal said still trying to sooth me.

"No, Jamal. That bitch tried to embarrass me in front of all these people, and I'm not about to let him get away with this." I replied in a harsh tone.

"Dae'Mon, you need to stop acting like a child! David is beneath you. You cannot allow people like that to get to you, otherwise you'll be miserable for the rest of your life. Now, pull yourself together!" Jamal said in a stern voice.

"See, I knew this wasn't a good idea! I know he's going make up lies to tell Milton. I'm ready to go, Jamal."

I was angry with myself for getting into that predicament. I wanted to go home because I knew the floodgates were going to open once Milton returned home.

Jamal paid the bill and escorted me out of the building. We walked to the car in silence. I was too busy thinking about Milton. I was afraid to lose him. Jamal finally broke the silence as we drove up Main St.

"Dae'Mon, what are you so afraid of?"

"I'm just afraid that I'm going to lose Milton. That's all." I responded.

"Dae'Mon listen. You and Milton just started seeing each other; and if he doesn't have anymore trust in you than to think that you're cheating on him, then maybe you should reevaluate your relationship with him. Without trust, there is nothing."

"There's a lot you don't understand."

"Oh you've been hurt before and you don't want to experience that again. You haven't found a good man until you met Milton. You're feeling good about yourself, right? I got the soundtrack and the sequel."

"It's not that simple, Jamal."

"Oh really! If you already fear Milton, then you are going to have some serious problems as time progresses. A good relationship is built on a solid foundation, and no one can tear that down. You don't need to surround yourself with Milton all the time. You need time to breathe and hang out with your friends on occasions. If he can't understand that, then he's a very insecure man and doesn't deserve to be with you." Jamal stated.

"Yeah, you're right..."

"I hear a "but" coming."

"But we just started seeing each other and I don't want to ruin it before it gets a chance to blossom."

"Dae'Mon, I'm gonna say one more thing about this situation and then I'm going to leave it alone. If it's meant to be, it's meant to be! If not, oh well!"

"Jamal, I really want to be your friend, but I'm afraid that Milton won't understand."

"Dae'Mon, I'm not going to beg for your friendship. If losing Milton is more important than a true friendship, then maybe we shouldn't be friends. I don't want to come between you and him. I just want to hang around good, quality people. Everyone excluding David has good things to say about you."

I didn't have a response. Everything Jamal said made perfect sense, but my insecurities were working overtime. I laid my head back on the seat with my eyes closed.

I had to digest everything he said to me. Jamal broke the silence again when we arrived at my loft.

"Dae'Mon, we're here."

I opened my eyes to see the front of my building. "Thank you for dinner, Jamal. I really appreciate all you've done." I said.

"Dae'Mon, you take care and learn how to love yourself."

With that said, I got out of the car and waved bye to Jamal. My speech had left me again. I watched him as he drove off. I let myself into my loft only to find Milton sitting on my sofa.

CHAPTER NINETEEN

Milton had a not so pleasing look on his face, which caused me to freeze in my tracks. All sorts of crazy things ran through my mind. I didn't have the strength to fight, but I could tell that a battle was ensuing. I tried to play it off.

"Milton sweetheart, what are you doing here?" I said as I walked towards him.

The appropriate question was how did he get into my loft. I never gave him a key. As curious as I was, I didn't dare ask him.

"No, the question is, what in the hell do you think you're doing?" He snapped.

I ignored the question. I didn't want to have it out with Milton, but I was losing my patience very quickly. I knew that bitch David had started some shit. But how did Milton get from St. Louis so quickly?

"I thought you weren't coming back until tomorrow morning?" I asked.

"Why? So you could have more time to ho around?" Milton snapped.

"What are you talking about?"

"I came back early, just hoping to spend time with my baby. And I get a phone call that you out with some other nigga. What's up with that Dae'Mon? Couldn't wait until I leave town to meet your tricks?"

"You wait one fucking minute! I'm not a got-damn whore! You best to check your sources and don't fall up in here starting shit with me." I said harshly.

Before I knew anything, Milton had grabbed me up by my collar. He began shaking me like I was a twig on a tree.

"Who the fuck do you think you talking to like that?"

"Milton, you're hurting me. Let me go." I screamed as I was trying to free myself from his grasp.

102

"You are mine Dae'Mon Greene. And I will not have you out in the streets acting like a tramp. Don't you ever speak to me again in that manner. Do I make myself clear?" Milton said through clenched teeth as he shook me violently with every word.

I was scared. Milton had the look of death in his eyes. I stopped resisting, hoping he would free me from his clutches. I was afraid to speak, but I knew I had to explain my position.

"Milton, darling…I haven't done anything. I was just having dinner with a friend. I would never disrespect you like that. You have to believe me!" I pleaded.

Milton pushed me down on the sofa and stood over me. I thought he was getting ready to tap dance on my head. I knew my tears would not phase him since he had fussed at me before about crying. So I was gonna take my ass whopping like a man.

He pointed his finger at me. "Dae'Mon, when I decided to get with you, I decided to put everyone else aside, and I expected for you to do the same thing. How could you betray me this way?"

"Milton baby, I promise you I didn't do anything wrong."

"Oh yeah, then what do you call making a scene in the restaurant and being out with another man? Just sipping on your tea?" Milton questioned.

"Milton, David Kelly came over fuc-…I mean messing with me at the table, and I had to tell him off. I knew he was going to start some mess. Baby, I promise I didn't do anything. I promise Milton. Please don't be mad." I said as I reached for him.

He knocked my hand away. "Dae'Mon, why were you out with another man?"

"Milton, I told you he is just someone that I know, and he knows all about me and you. I wouldn't jeopardize that for anything the world."

"Well you should have thought about that before you went out with him." Milton snapped.

"Milton, I don't mean any disrespect, but you are taking someone else's word over mine. If you can't trust me to do right by you, then why are you with me?" I questioned.

If looks could kill, I would have been dead.

"Dae'Mon, you're right. I did come over here and attack you. I apologize for that, but as long as you're mine, you will do as I say. You understand?" He questioned with authority.

"Milton, how does that sound? I'm a grown man." I retorted.

"Dae'Mon, I'm your man right?"

"Yes."

"Then act like it and stop talking back so much. You respect my manhood."

"Milton, what am I chopped liver?" I asked.

Milton walked over to where I was sitting. I jumped thinking he was about to hit me.

"Dae'Mon, why do you always have to have the last word? I'm your man. Now drop it!" He said forcefully.

I wasn't very happy with Milton's statement, but I wasn't about to press my luck. I dropped the subject against my better judgement.

"Are you still mad at me?" I asked with caution.

"Dae'Mon Greene. I don't know what you were up to this evening, but I'm here to tell you that before you pull another stunt like this, you had best to let me know. Clear?" He asked sternly.

"Yes, crystal clear."

"Good, I'm glad you finally understand, and you had better lose some of that smart mouth of yours before you find yourself in a world of trouble."

Milton placed his hand around my chin shaking me like I was a child. Under normal circumstances, I would have gone off, but Milton had me scared stiff. I sat there looking at him.

"Milton, I'm sorry if I upset you. I never meant to disrespect you. Please forgive me!"

"You're forgiven baby. Now come here and give daddy some love." Milton said as he pulled me closer and began to passionately kiss my lips.

The kiss burned deep inside. I could feel my temperature rising and my love tool coming to life. Milton drew back.

"I hope you enjoyed that." He asked.

"Yes very much so." I responded as I went for his lips again.

Milton held me in place. Looked into my eyes.

"Good, now you know what you'll be missing if you ever pull another stunt like that again." He said as he got up and walked out the door.

I ran after him. I didn't want him to leave.

"Milton, where are you going?" I asked trying to catch my breath.

"You have seen enough of me tonight. I'll be back to pick you up in the morning. Luv you. Bye, Bye!" He said as he got into his car and drove off.

"No!" I screamed.

I felt defeated. I was always told that I was going to meet my match one day. That day came when I met Milton Parker. I went inside, got in bed and cried myself to sleep.

CHAPTER TWENTY

"Have you completely lost your mind?"

"No, I haven't lost my mind Caleb. I'm completely sane."

"You sure about that? I just can't believe you would allow him to talk to you in that manner in your own home."

"Well, I didn't feel like arguing over something I know I didn't do."

"Whether you did something or not isn't the question! He disrespected you. Dae'Mon, as much as you may think you like Milton, you're gonna have to put your foot down and let him know that you're not a child and he can't boss you around."

"You're right Caleb. I should have told him off. But…"

"Oh no, Miss Thing…don't you dare give me any "butts"! You should have put his ass in check. I hope you're taking notes on all of this. This man is controlling, and you need to ask yourself, is this something you're willing to put up with?"

"Caleb."

"Look, I'm not trying to hurt you Dae'Mon, but you need to recognize when a man wants to run your life. I had a man like that, and my life was pure hell! I still have some battle marks to prove it. I thought I was in love, and I compromised on my principles. I lived my life the way he saw fit. I couldn't eat, shit or breathe without his permission. That's where I went wrong."

"I understand Caleb. I really do."

"You are one of the strongest men I know. Never allow another person to dictate your every move."

"Caleb, I will talk to Milton about this. I promise."

"Don't make promises you can't keep!"

"What does that suppose to mean?"

"It means Miss Thing that you are not going to talk to Milton about this because you are afraid he might leave you, and you will never get the chance to know what Milton Parker is all about."

"You can really be a bitch at times!"

"Whatever! You know I'm right. That's why you're angry. I'm just telling you what I know. Just be careful Dae'Mon! I don't want to see you hurt again like you were when Winton left. Remember?"

All too well!

—

It was during the fall semester of my sophomore year of college at the University of Kansas when I found my second relationship. I was at the enrollment center signing up for additional classes when I caught a glimpse of a gorgeous specimen standing in the line behind me. His beauty mesmerized me. He was about 6'1" 175 pounds of brawn with full lips and beautiful eyes that complimented his chiseled chocolate brown face.

I stared at him for about ten minutes before he looked up and caught me staring at him. He smiled and nodded. I nodded and thought to myself that he had a beautiful smile. Suddenly, I became embarrassed that I had been caught in the act. What would he think of me? I thought to myself. I was very happy that I was the next person in line so I could quickly escape. Although I didn't know him from Adam, he had me in a trance, and I didn't need to be in that state.

I enrolled for my classes and tried to make a quick exit through the large wooden doors at the back of Strong Hall. To my surprise, the mystery guy was sitting on a bench just to the left of the sidewalk. I put my head down studying the configurations of the concrete under my feet trying not to look in his direction. He rose to his feet and strolled up to me. He extended his hand and introduced himself. "My name is Winton Tucker, Jr. from Charlotte, North Carolina," he said.

I was in utter shock. It took a moment before my heart stopped palpitating and breathing returned to normal. As I began to speak, my voice cracked. I cleared my throat and properly introduced myself. My palms began to sweat as I thought Winton would think that I was a freak for dissecting him with my eyes.

Winton rescued me from my state of panic by saying that he had noticed me in line and wanted to chat with me. I tried to play it cool by saying that he looked lost standing in line, and that's why I was looking at him. Liar!

Winton went on to tell me that he transferred to KU from North Carolina A & T.

He said he was tired of his parents trying to run his life, and he wanted a fresh start. So, he decided to attend KU due to the Journalism Program being ranked #1 in the country.

While Winton was speaking, I began to fantasize about making love with him. I could feel the heat that would be generated from our bodies' rhythmic motion. I could taste his juicy lips pressed against mine while we caressed each other gently. I guess I got a little too involved in my fantasy as I could feel my lovetool beginning to rise. Oops! I knew I was tripping. I didn't know this man nor did I know if he was in the life.

I snapped out of it but not before Winton asked me if I was ok. I lied and said that I was just thinking about something that I had to take care of later that afternoon. Winton then asked me if I would join him for lunch. I said yes without hesitation.

Winton and I went to the student union for lunch. I was still somewhat in shock that I was sitting across from the man that I had lusted after just a short time before. I guess that dreamy lustful look had returned to my eyes. Winton asked me what was I thinking about? I had to think of a quick lie. I said that I was just thinking about one of my friends from school. He had a puzzled look on his face, and said it must have been a very special friend..." Just what does that suppose to mean?" I said. He responded by saying that I had a look of love and romance in my eyes. Little did he know!

I knew which direction the conversation was heading. I excused myself from the table. But before I could escape, Winton asked for my phone number. I wrote my number on a napkin as he wrote his number on a piece of paper that he retrieved from his wallet. Winton told me that he would call me later that afternoon to see if we could meet for dinner. I said ok and I left to go home.

I didn't understand why I was so afraid. After all, I was the one who was staring at him like a lovesick fool. I thought about it and realized that it was because of the hurt factor. If I could hold on to my fantasy about him, then I wouldn't have to worry about being hurt. The problem was that he was lusting after me just as much as I was lusting after him. I wasn't sure what I was going to do if he made a move.

My fear became a reality when like clockwork Winton called just as he said he would. I accepted a dinner date with him. I was nervous yet excited. I was nervous because I knew I wouldn't be able to resist him and could possibly get hurt again. I was excited because I would be in the arms of a fine man.

We decided to get together later that evening at Winton's apartment. He bragged about being a good cook. I had always loved a man who knew his way around a kitchen. Needless to say I didn't object to meeting at his place.

When I arrived at Winton's apartment, he had a huge smile on his face. He had the table beautifully decorated with a candle burning in the middle to lighten the mood. I was giddy. I let out a squeal when Winton brought the food to the table. He prepared stuffed pork chops, scalloped potatoes, green beans and fresh baked bread. Dinner was delicious. I thanked him for preparing dinner and told him that he would make someone a good husband one-day. He responded by saying that he would like to be my husband. I was dumbfounded. I couldn't believe what I was hearing.

I played dumb and said, "What do you mean?" He gave me a look that said don't play dumb with me. When he finally spoke, he said, "Dae'Mon I saw the lust in your eyes at lunch." I was speechless. I just sat there and didn't say anything. Winton suddenly got up and kissed me on the lips. How do I describe the kiss? It was all that I had imagined and more. It was a soft kiss filled with so much passion that sent sparks through my body. Me and my sparks!

Well to make a long story short, Winton and I started a love affair that lasted until the end of our senior year of college. Just like with Edwin, he promised that we would be together after we graduated. On the day I thought would be the happiest day of my life, I was run over by that train again.

During the graduation ceremony, Winton whispered in my ear that he was moving back to North Carolina to attend graduate school. I asked him when were we leaving? He said that I wouldn't like it there, and he didn't want me to be unhappy. I felt numb all over, and the rest of the ceremony was a blank. The only thing that I remember is that Caleb took me to dinner after the ceremony because Winton's family was in town, and he didn't want them to find out about us. I was so hurt not only because of what Winton did but because my family did not attend my graduation. My brother wanted to come, but he was playing in the commencement band at his own school. I cried all night and blew the interview I had scheduled for the following morning. Needless to say, I didn't get the job.

The graduation ceremony was the last I saw or heard from Winton. He left town the following day without a goodbye, a thank you or a kiss my ass! I really didn't understand what had transpired until Caleb told me that a friend of his informed him that Winton was lying about graduate school. It was reported that Winton had been messing around with a guy named Darren that he met during the fall semester, and they planned to move to Chicago together. Caleb went on to tell me that he had seen Winton several times on campus with this mysterious man. I didn't have a clue that this was going on. I asked Caleb why he didn't tell me, and he said that he tried but I wouldn't listen. So, he stayed out of it. I started feeling numb again. Winton was so attentive and adorable to me. I just couldn't believe he would do this! I cried again all night and vowed I would never love again.

—

"Hey, I was just calling to check on you. You seemed pretty upset after I dropped you off."

"Thanks for calling Jamal. I appreciate your concern. But I don't think it's a good idea for me to talk to you right now."

"Why is that?"

"Because Milton came back early from St. Louis; and just as I had predicted, that bitch David called his house and told him I was out with another man. Needless to say Milton was livid and went off on me."

"Well, I'm sorry to hear about that Dae'Mon. I never meant to cause you any pain. I'm just trying to make new friends in this new city. That's all."

"Yes, but I don't think I'm the friend that you need. I have some issues I need to clear up with Milton before I can proceed, and I really don't need any distractions to cloud my thoughts. I think that you are a great guy, but you deserve true friends. Right now, I don't think I can be a true friend to you."

"Dae'Mon, it sounds to me as if Milton has frightened you into thinking that your world revolves around him. That's not a healthy relationship. You need friends outside of your mate. Lord knows you do!"

"What does that suppose to mean?"

"Well, you have been friends with that guy Kevyn for years, and he has not been a true friend to you. I hear that the only true friends you have are Caleb and Justice. I just want to be a part of your circle of friends because I hear that you are such a great person."

"Where do you get your information? You seem to know my life story." I laughed nervously.

"You're very popular in this city. Not to mention good looking! I can tell that you're a great guy." Jamal responded.

"I don't know about that Jamal. I don't want to think about anything right now. I'm sorry but I really need to go. You will be successful in finding good friends. I'm not the only nice guy in town."

"Dae'Mon, if that's what you want, I will respect your decision. However, I want you to just be aware of the fact that I'm trying to reach out to you as a friend only. That's all I really want from you."

"Why me Jamal? Out of all the guys in Kansas City, Why me?"

"Because you're genuine and true. Those are rare traits to find in people today. I got a good vibe from you when you came to the bar to get a drink that night. I have to admit that I was mesmerized by your beauty at first; but when you came near, I knew you were someone that I wanted to get to know more. I was told so many goods things about what type of person you are, and I knew my instincts were right."

"Jamal thank you so much for those kind words, but…"

"But what Dae'Mon? Milton is your man. I understand that, and I just want to be a friend. I need someone to show me around the city and hang out with on occasions."

"I'll tell you what. I need to talk to Milton to clear up some things and I'll let you know of my decision. Ok?"

"I guess that's fair enough. Dae'Mon, just remember one thing, good friends are hard to find. True friends will be there when the rest of the world has walked out."

So True.

CHAPTER TWENTY - ONE

Several weeks had passed since my car had been vandalized. Life returned to normal without further incident. It had also been several weeks since Milton chastised me for going to dinner with Jamal. I tried to talk to him about his behavior, but he wouldn't listen. He would always change the subject, so I decided to just leave it alone for the time being. I knew the opportunity would present itself sooner or later.

It occurred at a Valentine's Day Party we had been invited to at one of Milton's colleague's house. Milton was in the kitchen talking to a co-worker. I was sitting in the living room listening to three queens talking about everyone arriving at the party. They did not have a kind word to say about anyone. I was not amused.

Neither one had room to talk about anyone, especially the ringleader, Roosevelt. Roosevelt was about three hundred pounds and smelled of day old mustard greens. His clothes were too tight to fit his body, but you couldn't tell him that he didn't look good. Please! He had bug eyes that made him look like a bullfrog in drag. He was definitely a sight for sore eyes.

I had enough of their buffoonery, so I decided to excuse myself to join Milton. I got up from the sofa and was headed toward the kitchen. Roosevelt seized the opportunity to be vicious.

"What's the matter Prissy can't handle the heat?" Roosevelt questioned as he and his posse laughed.

I could feel my body going numb. My central nervous system was shutting down. It was on! I stopped in my tracks and turned around to face the hog in human clothing. "Excuse me!" I said harshly.

"You too good to be around us? We too alley for you?"

"I like to be around intelligent conversation, not a bunch of old loud mouth washed-up queens who get a thrill out of slamming people."

"Oh, no you didn't! You scrawny little bitch! You ain't all that cuz yo man is a lawyer!"

A crowd had begun to gather around the festivities. The kids were always up for a good reading session. I didn't see it that way. I saw it as a personal attack on my character just because I was dating Milton.

"Bitch puh-leeze! I would much rather being scrawny than sitting over there looking like a pork roast. Unlike you, I don't need a man to define who I am! As if you could get a man in the first place!

The crowd roared in laughter. I wanted to laugh, but I had work that needed to be completed. I was preparing to shut that cow down for good.

"Bitch, I will come over there and whip your little bean pole ass!"

"I like to see that. You'd be out of breath before you made it over here." I said as Milton grabbed my arm.

"Dae'Mon, what's going on?" Milton questioned.

"I'm about to whip your little bitch's ass." Roosevelt said as he stood up.

"What you gonna do? Sit on me?" I replied.

The crowd roared in laughter again. Milton gave me an "I'm gonna get you" look. I didn't care. I wasn't about to stand there and allow that fool to dis me.

"Dae'Mon, that's enough!" Milton yelled.

Milton put his hand on the small of my back and pushed me through the crowd into the kitchen. I was laughing to myself, but I didn't want Milton to know I was amused. He wouldn't have been pleased. I had to give Roosevelt a taste of his own medicine, and when I did, he didn't know what to do.

"You need to feed that anorexic bitch!" Roosevelt yelled from the living room.

"Roosevelt I have two words for you, Jenny Craig." I yelled back from the kitchen.

"Dae'Mon, I said that's enough. You're embarrassing me!" Milton said sternly.

I was furious. I couldn't believe the only thing that concerned him was me embarrassing him when his co-worker verbally assaulted me.

"Oh really! I'm embarrassing you? How dare you stand there and yell at me when that bitch started in on me? Was I not suppose to defend myself?" I questioned.

"You acting ghetto." Milton responded.

I could feel the blood rushing to my head. As far as I was concerned, it was all out war.

"Now I'm ghetto. If I'm so fucking ghetto, why in hell are you with me?" I yelled.

"Let's take this outside." Milton said as he snatched me by my hand. "I warned you about your mouth didn't I?" Milton said as we stood on the porch.

"You warned me! You are not my father, Milton Parker, and I will not stand here and allow you to disrespect me like you did back in January. I'm a grown man and you will treat me as such."

Milton grabbed me up by my collar. His eyes were blood shot red. If I didn't know any better, I could have sworn I saw smoke coming out of his ears.

"Don't you ever talk to me that way again! Understand?" Milton said through clenched teeth.

I wasn't afraid this time. Well at least I wasn't going to let on.

"Milton, I will ask you nicely to release me."

"Or what Dae'Mon? What you gonna do?"

"Milton, let me go!" I said as I tried to free myself. "I can see now that you have a control problem. I'm not one of your clients nor am I a child! I will not be insulted!"

Milton released me from his grasp. I stood there glaring at him wanting to steal on him, but I didn't want to stoop that low.

"Milton, I think it's best that you take me home now."

"We will go when I say we can go!" Milton snapped.

"Who died and made you king of the world? I'm ready to go, now! Fuck it, I'll just walk home!" I said as I turned to walk away.

Milton grabbed me and spun me around. He raised a clenched fist up to my face. I braced myself for the blow.

"I told you about your mouth."

"Milton, if you hit me, as God as my witness I will meet your soul in hell!" I said although I was scared stiff.

Milton pushed me so hard that I almost fell off the porch. I gathered myself and walked away.

"Where do you think you're going?" Milton questioned.

"I'm going home. I have had enough of you! You're crazy!" I said.

Milton came behind me and I started running. Milton chased me down the street. I was able to lose him thanks to my superior track skills. I hid behind a bush until Milton had passed. After about fifteen minutes, he eventually gave up his search for me. When I felt the coast was clear, I started walking.

I didn't know how I was going to get home. The party was held in Grandview, and I lived downtown. I saw a gas station several blocks away. I headed in that direction to call Justice to come pick me up. Just as I began to dial the phone, Milton drove up.

I was too frightened to run. I felt like a deer caught in headlights. Milton parked the car, got out and walked over to me.

"Get in!" He ordered.

"No! It's over between us. I don't want to see you again."

Milton grabbed me around my waist and looked into my eyes. "You're not leaving me. I will never let you go."

"Milton, I'm not the one for you. You want someone that you can control, and that's not me. I would much rather die before I allow someone to rule over me." I stated.

"Dae'Mon, you're mine. I love you and you're not leaving me." He said as he began to kiss me.

"No." I said trying to separate my lips from his.

The harder I tried to push Milton away, the harder and passionately he kissed me. I could feel myself being reeled in. I finally surrendered to him. We kissed and kissed.

I was thankful it was late and no one was around or better yet the police didn't arrive.

"I'm sorry baby. I lost my head and I never should have yelled at you." Milton said still holding me around my waist.

"No, you shouldn't have Milton. You disrespected me."

"I know baby. I promise I will make it up to you."

With that said, we climbed in the car and Milton drove off. We rode in silence just holding hands listening to the sounds of Natalie Cole's Inseparable on the radio. How appropriate!

Yes, I gave in to Milton. However, I earned his respect that night. Don't give me that! You would have done the same thing.

Instead of going back to my place, Milton headed toward the plaza where his condo was located.

CHAPTER TWENTY - TWO

Milton had taken me to his condo several times before, but I always found myself amazed every time I went. I never wanted to touch anything or go anywhere in fear of messing something up. His place was beautifully decorated and exceptionally clean. I was neat and tidy, but my place didn't have anything on his. The floors were so clean; you could eat off it. I kid you not! Milton assured me that it was no big deal, and I should make myself at home. I never could. I felt out of place.

Don't get me wrong, I made good money working for IST; but it was obvious that my salary was pocket change to Milton. He told me over and over again that he wasn't materialistic and none of those things meant as much to him as I did. I was still intimidated.

How would you feel? The condo was located on the Plaza, which told you it was expensive. The building where the condo was located looked like a big English Cathedral. I felt as if I was going into a church. Luxury oozed from every brick that made up the foundation of this building.

Milton occupied 4000 square feet of living space, which included three bedrooms, three and half bathrooms, a library, a rec. room, a private office, family room, living room, a home theatre center, a state of the art kitchen with a bar and closets which seemed larger than my bedroom. These rooms were strategically situated throughout this two-level condo. I forgot there was area in the back of the condo just in case he wanted a live-in servant. I felt like a fish out of water.

On top of that, the furnishing in his place was top of the line as if he bought it from Jennifer Convertibles or some other expensive store. Milton would always say, "It's just stuff." There wasn't anything he could say to ever make me feel comfortable. He would get angry with me for always trying to find an excuse to keep from going there.

When we turned on to Brush Creek heading to his condo, I tried to worm my way out of going.

"Milton, I need to go home." I said.

"Why?"

"I just want to check on my car."

"You're car is fine. Dae'Mon, I don't know why you never like to come to my place. What are you so afraid of?"

"Nothing." I lied.

"Oh really! Then explain to me why you always suddenly need something from your place whenever I suggest we come back to mine." Milton stated.

I had been busted. I was rendered speechless because I didn't have a good excuse. "Well, I'm waiting." He said with a "make it a good one" look on his face.

"Milton, I never feel comfortable there. I feel as if I don't belong there, like I'm out of my league. I know it's silly, but that's how I feel."

"Well Dae'Mon, you best to get use to it because this is where you'll be living soon."

I was shocked with Milton's revelation. He had a smug smile on his face.

"When did I decide to do this?" I asked.

"You didn't. Where else is my future husband going to live?"

"Milton, did I miss something?"

"No, you haven't missed a thing. I just think it would be appropriate to have you live here when we get married. Besides, you're renting the place where you live and I own this one. It will then become ours after we say I do."

"I would appreciate it that in the future, you discuss things with me before you make a final decision for me. You may not be good enough for me to marry." I joked.

"Don't play me like that. You know you can't get enough of me." He laughed.

"You always say that, but I think you fail to realized that you can't get enough of me either. No pun intended but you have been hooked for over three years."

"Yeah, yeah! I may have, but you have been drooling over me for just as long."

We laughed.

"I don't know what you're talking about."

"Of course not, the record speaks for itself. Milton said as he placed his hand on top of mine. "Baby, come on, I have a surprise for you."

"What is it?"

"Then it wouldn't be a surprise." Milton said as he planted little kisses on my hand.

"Ok, I'll go, but no funny business. You stay on your side of the bed." I said as I removed my hand from his lips.

"I promise. I'll be the perfect gentleman."

Milton turned into the highly secured parking garage. There was a security checkpoint at a guard station to keep the undesirables out. I had never seen anything like that before. You could tell I wasn't use to anything. Country boy!

As soon as we made it to the condo, Milton grabbed me. We made love in the middle of the floor and again when we made it upstairs to the bedroom.

We laid in bed recovering from our love making when Milton handed me a gold box.

"What's this?" I questioned.

"You're future." Milton responded.

I opened the box to find a key and a clearance badge. I was somewhat puzzled until it hit me what Milton had said earlier.

"Milton, I don't understand."

"This key is to the condo and the badge is so you can get into the garage."

"But why Milton? We've known each for other only a short time."

"Dae'Mon, I want to spend the rest of my life with you. So why waste time? Tomorrow is not promised to any of us, and that's why I'm not waiting another minute. I know how I feel about you, and I just hope you feel the same way about me." Milton said with tears welding up in his eyes.

"Milton Parker, I love you. I will accept these things from the bottom of my heart. I thank you for loving me, and I will do my best to make sure our love never dies." I said as I leaned over and kissed his face.

"Thank you Dae'Mon! I love you so much! Happy Valentine's Day, baby." Milton said as he handed me another small box.

"Milton, what is this? You sure are full of surprises this morning," I said as I opened the box.

My mouth flew open I saw a diamond ring shining at me. A five-carat diamond ring with a gold ban. I was speechless. I laid my head on Milton's chest just staring at the ring.

In the words of Faith Evans, I Never Knew A Love Like This Before. Tears flowed down Milton's face as he caressed my hand.

"Oh My God! I can't believe you. I'm not worth all of this." I said.

"Baby, you are worth this and more. I love you!"

We kissed and cried and kissed and cried. I put the ring on my finger. It was a perfect fit. I chuckled thinking about how Milton tricked me into giving him one of my rings to get my ring size, but it didn't' matter anymore. I felt special.

I went to sleep in Milton's arms with a big smile on my face.

CHAPTER TWENTY - THREE

Nine months had passed and my relationship with Milton was still going strong. Milton touched emotions in me that I never knew existed. I deserted my fears of falling in love and in turn loved with reckless abandon.

I was feeling good about myself. My life had taken a turn for the better, and I was looking forward to living happily ever after with Milton.

Justice and Jamal were very supportive of my relationship, and Milton and I even hung out together with them on occasions. Milton grew to become very fond of Jamal. I was surprised because I thought Milton would be jealous of my friendship with him. If he were, he never showed any signs of it when he was with me. Caleb came to visit, and he and Milton had a blast. I was happy even though my relationship with Kevyn had turned very ugly.

My car was vandalized again. Someone scratched the words "Die Fucking Bitch!" on the hood all the way through the paint. I was so upset about the incident that I didn't think twice when Milton asked if he could take care of everything. He wanted to capture the perpetrator, so I wouldn't have to worry about my car being damaged again. Unbeknownst to me, Milton had a surveillance camera installed to monitor the car.

In was during the summer in late August when the surveillance camera recorded Kevyn spray painting my car with black paint. It destroyed the sky blue color on the car. I was devastated. Milton was livid and wanted Kevyn to rot in jail. Subsequently, Kevyn was arrested and charged with vandalism.

Milton chewed me a new one because I refused to press charges. As mad as I was, I didn't want Kevyn to spend any time in jail. After of lot of convincing, Milton agreed not to peruse charges. However, he wanted Kevyn to be punished, so he convinced the District Attorney to give Kevyn a $1,000 fine and a year's probation. Kevyn never called to say thank you, even though the DA wanted to charge him with a felony.

I soon put the ordeal to the side and concentrated on my life with Milton. I was happy again.And what was more amazing was the fact that Justice had finally found a good man who treated her well. She was happy and in good spirit. She deserved it.

I was even more surprised when Milton said he wanted to go to Mississippi to visit my family. We scheduled our trip for the Thanksgiving Holiday.

I was overjoyed and things were going too well, so I should have known that life was about to bring about a change. I just didn't realize how big!

CHAPTER TWENTY - FOUR

I was flying on the wings of love. Milton pampered me and continuously showered me with gifts. Each passing day, my feelings were becoming deeper for him, and he seemed to be feeling the same way about me.

I later realized that the special treatment was Milton's way of saying he wanted me to move in with him. As much as I wanted to, I knew that it was too soon to make that decision. I still had three more months left on my lease, so I figured that would be a good time to make a move if things were still going strong. Milton was very understanding and didn't pressure me. That made me feel good.

I went to work on Cloud 9. I was even pleasant to my annoying secretary, Agnes. Can you believe that? She looked at me as if I was crazy. I normally grumbled at her when she spoke to me, but I had a spring in my step that morning. I strolled to my office preparing to start my day, refusing to allow anything to bother me. I had just entered my office when the phone ranged. I knew it was Agnes calling to bother me.

"This is Dae'Mon."

"Hey baby, I was just calling to say I love you." Milton said.

"You're too sweet. I love you too. You always seem to call me when I just walk through the door. You got a camera in here or something?" I joked.

"Yeah, you don't see it?" Milton laughed.

"Don't be spying on me. I like to sit at my desk in the nude."

"You better not be showing off what's mine. I don't want to come up there and cut anybody."

We laughed.

"Ok, I'll put my clothes back on. I can't wait to see you this evening."

"I can't wait to see you. I gotta go my love, but I'll call you later."

"Ok, I miss you already."

"I know you do." Milton laughed. "I miss you too, talk to you later."

I had a huge smile on my face after my conversation with Milton. He sure knew how to make me feel good. I had it bad for him, real bad. I missed him when we weren't together, and I got excited just thinking about seeing him. True love!

I tried to concentrate on my work but to no avail. I couldn't stop thinking about Milton. Every time my phone ranged, I prayed it was him. It wasn't, always work related. After an hour of lustful thoughts, I mustered up enough concentration to work on a report for a client. I was nearing completion when the phone ranged.

"Yes Agnes!" I said.

"I have a call for you. She says it's urgent." Agnes said.

"Who is it?" I asked.

"She wouldn't tell me."

"Ok, well take a message and I'll call her back. Thanks Agnes." I said as I hung up the phone.

I started on my report when the phone beeped again. I was going to let Agnes have it for disturbing me.

"Yes Agnes!" I said slightly agitated.

"Mr. Greene, she said she wants to talk to you now. It's your mother."

"Fine, send it through."

The call was transferred to my desk. I started to let it go to my voice mail. Why would my mother call and not identify herself? I didn't buy it for one minute.

"IST, this is Dae'Mon Greene."

"Dae'Mon, this is your mother."

"Ma, why didn't you tell Agnes who you were? I don't take calls unless the party is identified." I said.

"That little witch was nasty to me, but that's not why I called. Dae'Mon, you need to come home immediately. Big Mama is in the hospital. The doctors are not expecting for her to live."

I knew my ears were deceiving me. I felt numb all over. My speech failed me. Big Mama couldn't be close to death. No!

"Dae'Mon, you there?" Mother asked.

"Yeah Ma, I'm here. Ma what happened?" I questioned.

"I'll explain everything when you get here."

"I'll be there as soon as I can. I'll call you with my flight information. Are you at home?"

"No, I'm at the hospital on your daddy's cell phone."

"Ok, I'll call you back in a few minutes." I said as I hung up the phone.

I called my travel agent and booked a flight to Memphis for 1:00 that afternoon. Memphis was the closest city to the town where I grew up that had an airport. Mother was softly sobbing when I called, and that didn't help matters. My mind was running in circles, and I was losing control fast. I tried to calm myself. I was shaking like a leaf and going into shock.

I left the office heading home. I wanted to pack and call Milton. My hands were shaking so that I couldn't dial Milton's work number. I remembered I had it programmed into my cell phone. I hit the speed dial button.

"Bradley, Emerson and Parker Law Firm, how may I direct your call?" The voice said.

"Milton Parker please."

"May I ask whose calling?"

"Yes, this is Dae'Mon Greene."

"One moment please." The female voice said as I was placed on hold to the sound of music.

Elevator music. I hated elevator music. A big time law firm playing cheap music. Yuck! My thoughts were interrupted by the receptionist voice.

"Mr. Greene, I'm sorry but Mr. Parker is in with a client."

"It's urgent that I speak with him at once." I stated.

"I'm sure it is! Everyone always has emergencies, but you'll just have to wait." The receptionist said harshly.

"Bitch, who the fuck you think you're talking to? You get Mr. Parker on the phone right now." I demanded.

Ms. Dial Tone serenaded my ear. I wasn't amused to say the least. I couldn't' hit the redial button fast enough.

"Bradley, Emerson and Parker Law Firm, How may I direct your call?"

"What is your name?"

"Felice."

"Felice what?" I asked.

"I'm not allowed to give out my last name."

"Whatever! I'll be there in a few minutes and I'll make sure Mr. Parker has your ass for your fucked up attitude." I said as I hit the power button on my phone.

I decided to try Milton's cell phone. He always had his cell phone on his hip. I hit the speed dial button and got Milton's voice mail. I didn't have much time, so I left a message.

"Milton, this is Dae'Mon. I'm leaving for Mississippi in two hours. My grandmother is on her deathbed. I will call you once I get there. By the way, you need to do something with that receptionist, Felice. She was very rude to me, and I don't appreciate it. I love you and I'll talk to you soon." I stated as I clicked the power button.

I sped home and packed whatever I saw. I didn't have time to be fashionable. Big Mama needed me. I got to the airport about five minutes before boarding. I was depressed and out of breath. I slept through the hour and half flight and didn't wake up until the plane landed in Memphis.

CHAPTER TWENTY - FIVE

I arrived at Memphis International Airport at 2:30 that afternoon. I was tired and groggy from my restless sleep on the plane. My mind was in a state of confusion. I didn't understand how a woman who was the picture of health could be knocking on death's door. Of all the things that could go wrong, I sure didn't want it to be the death of Big Mama. She was the only member of my family who loved me for who I was other than my brother, Marshall. They were my anchor until I moved away to attend college. I didn't know what I would do if she passed away.

She would always tell me that during adversity you would see your greatest strength. At the time, I didn't understand what she meant by that statement. I finally understood. I would need that strength because I was getting weak. I knew my mother would be an emotional wreck, and my father would play the tough guy role.

Big Mama had always been the stable force in our family. She came to live with us when I was 8 years old and had been there ever since. She was a very strong willed woman who took great pride in raising six boys on her own after the death of her husband. She never remarried. I could hear her now saying, "A woman ain't pose to love but one man." I smiled just thinking about that because you know I loved more than one man and was falling in love with another one at that time.

I was overjoyed when Big Mama came to live with us. We needed someone to put my daddy in his place. My father, Levi Greene, was a stubborn man and bitter toward life. Big Mama said it was due to his anger over his father's death when he was 10 years old. He was never the same after that, so he took his anger out on me and occasionally my brother. Big Mama saved Marshall and me from several tongue-lashings. We were grateful. My mother would sit there and wouldn't say a word. She and Big Mama had several battles over us kids- Marshall, my sister Lisa and me.

Big Mama would always chastise my mother for allowing my daddy to verbally abuse us. She would say, "Sharon, it don't make sense for a mother to sit by and let a man talk bad bout her kids. It just ain't right." My mother would walk away. I resented her for years because I felt she didn't do enough to protect me from my father's wrath.

I was never good enough in his sight. I graduated valedictorian of my high school class and graduated with highest distinction from Kansas, but I was not a real man to him because I was gay. I gave up trying to please my daddy. I figured that his anger was too far-gone, so I began living my life for me. I stopped visiting and only called my parents on special occasions such as Mother's Day, Thanksgiving and Christmas. I regretted not visiting more because Big Mama was my world. I would call and talk to her all the time. She understood why though, so there was no explanation needed.

Big Mama told me that if I wouldn't come to her; she would come to me. She convinced Marshall to bring her to Kansas City on several occasions. We were like three peas in a pod. I enjoyed their company so much and always hated when they left.

I had butterflies in my stomach. This was the first time I had been back to my hometown in five years. The painful memories of my childhood kept me away. I didn't want to face my daddy or Edwin who still resided in Pecan Grove.

After I walked through the boarding gates, I was pleasantly surprised to see my brother, Marshall, waiting for me. Although I was three years older, Marshall and I could pass for twins. We looked exactly alike and were about the same height. I had maybe an inch on him, but most people could never tell us apart.

He had a huge smile on his face when he saw me. My smile grew even bigger. Marshall was one of my best friends. He met me at the terminal and gave me a big hug.

"Wassup big brother?" Marshall said still holding on to me.

"I'm so happy to see you. How are you holding up?"

"I'm cool, just worried about Big Mama." He said finally releasing me.

"Well she'll be fine. I'm here now."

"You're staying with me right?" Marshall asked.

"Yeah. I am."

"Good. Let's go get your stuff from baggage claim."

We retrieved my luggage from baggage claim and headed to Marshall's gold 98 Honda Accord. I was proud of Marshall and his accomplishments. He graduated from college with honors and went on to teach chemistry at Coahoma Junior College located in a town about 16 miles east of where we grew up.

I have to admit it that our looks were not the only thing that I thought Marshall and I had in common. Marshall never married or dated anyone that I knew of. He spent most of his time with his best friend, Finus Davis. I figured if he were like me, he would eventually tell me when the time was right.

"Marshall, what happened to Big Mama?" I questioned as I got in the car.

"Well, the doctors say that she has swelling on the brain which is causing her to remain unconscious."

"What's causing the swelling?"

"That's just it! They don't know. They say that all of her vital signs are good. I'm really worried D." Marshall said with tears in his eyes.

"I just don't understand. Did this happen today?" I said as I wiped his eyes.

"Yeah, this morning around 6:30. Ma found her lying on the floor."

131

"Oh my God! How is Ma holding up?"

"D, she's doing the best that she can. She looks very worn and I'm sure she will be glad to see you."

"Where's daddy?"

"He's at the hospital with Ma."

"What hospital is she in?" I asked.

"Clarksdale Regional Hospital. We'll go there first and then I'll take you to my house."

"Ok, that sounds like a winner. Where is Ms. Lisa?"

"Ma called her, but I'm not sure if she's coming. She lives in Jackson now. That girl has changed so much since you left. She thinks that she is better than all of us. I can't tell you the last time I've seen her."

My sister, Lisa, married a doctor from Jackson and turned up her nose at everyone in the family. She said that they were all country and ass backwards. She severed all ties with me because she said I was an eye sore in the sight of God because I was gay.

Big Mama gave her an earful for her behavior at the last family reunion in which I conveniently was not in attendance. Marshall gave me the dirt on how Big Mama told Lisa that she wasn't shit just because she married a doctor. Lisa got so mad that she and her doctor husband burned rubber getting away and hadn't been back to town since. Served her right for looking down at everyone!

"Well, I'm sure she won't be happy to see the eye sore of the family." I said.

"Forget her! She's an idiot for selling her soul to the devil just to get money. That man doesn't love her. My friends in Jackson report that he beats her. How's that for happiness?"

"You lie! Well, hopefully if she comes, she'll act with class."

"Well, she shouldn't come then. I'm concerned about Big Mama's health and not in the mood for Lisa's shit." Marshall snapped.

The family felt that Lisa was a snob and didn't want her around them. She would put them down and brag and boast about the house the doctor bought her and all the other fine things she owned. They were not amused.

"Marshall, when are you going to move away from here?" I questioned.

"I can't leave now. Big Mama is the only reason why I never strayed that far from home. If she leaves this world, I will definitely move away."

"Oh yeah! Where would you move?"

"I'll have to come up there and show my big brother how to live it up in the big city."

We laughed.

"Marshall, you know Big Mama is proud of you just like I am?"

"Yeah, I know and that's why I can't leave her here, and I know she wouldn't move away with me. I just can't stand the fact that she lives in that house with daddy."

"He's her son though, and she knows her child better than we do."

"Yeah but she deserves to be happy and peaceful. There's no peace in that house with that man."

"Well, when she gets better, you can ask her to move away with you. I'm sure she will do it."

"How do you know she will be ok?"

"Because I prayed and I know the Lord is not going to take my Big Mama away from me. I just know he won't, so that's why I'm not worried." I said confidently.

"Well, I just hope you're right." He said as he placed his hand on my shoulder.

I laid the seat back and closed my eyes and prayed again for Big Mama's speedy recovery. I dozed off. Marshall gently shook me when we arrived at the hospital. It was time for me to use that strength. I would need it seeing Big Mama and facing my daddy.

I was ready.

J. Aundre Clinton

CHAPTER TWENTY - SIX

As if Marshall and I weren't already gloomy, the paleness of the beige walls in the Intensive Care Unit made both of us even more depressed as we walked through the lobby. My stomach began to bubble, as I was becoming ill from the aroma of the ammonia that was used to clean the place. I was trying to be strong because I wanted to uplift my mother even though I didn't like being at the hospital. Hospitals reminded me of sickness and death.

As we approached the waiting area, I could see my mother sitting with her head on my daddy's chest as he sat with a stone face. My mother raised up as she saw us approaching. She quickly ran over to us.

"Baby, I'm so glad you made it." Mother said as she hugged me.

"How you holding up?" I asked.

"I'm ok I guess. I'm worried about your father." Mother said releasing her embrace.

"Ok, I'll go talk to him." I said as I hesitantly walked over to my father. I extended my hand to shake his. I wasn't going to press my luck in asking him for a hug. "That's "sissy shit," he would always say. He rose to his feet.

"Dae'Mon, thanks for coming. I'm sure Mama would appreciate that." He said as he shook and released my hand.

"Any word on what's wrong?"

"No, they're still running tests and not sure what's wrong with her."

"Daddy, how are you holding up?" I questioned.

"I'm doing as well as I can considering the circumstances. Thanks for asking."

"Ok, well I'm going to get situated and I'll be back."

"Ok, son."

I walked toward my mother and brother who were engaged in a small conversation. My mother had a very strained look on her face. She needed to rest.

"Ma, I'm going to go to Marshall's house and freshen up. Then, I'll come back so you and daddy can go home and rest."

"Baby, I appreciate it, but we want to stay here."

"Ma, I understand but if you two are tired and worn down you won't be any good for anyone. Please don't argue! I'm here now and we can share in staying."

"Ma, I agree with Dae'Mon. You should go rest." Marshall said.

"Ok, I'll talk to your father about it.

My mother walked over to my father and took a seat next to him. Marshall and I headed to the elevator. My parents didn't look good. Their faces were long and distressed. It saddened me to see them in that state.

"Marshall, what was Ma saying to you?"

"She was talking about there being no word on Big Mama's condition. She was worried that we were going to lose her."

"I'm not worried. Big Mama is a fighter, and she's gonna be just fine. We'll give them a break after we get back from your house. Ok?"

"Yeah, that's fine. I hope Lisa doesn't show up."

"That may be the best thing. The last thing we need is more stress." I said as I climbed into Marshall's car.

Marshall sped away from the hospital heading to his house on Big Field located in West Marks. I was nervous thinking that he would get a ticket as fast as he was driving. We made it to his house in a whopping 10 minutes.

As soon as Marshall turned into his driveway, my cell phone began to ring. I grabbed my briefcase and pulled out the phone.

"Hello." I said.

"Baby, this is Milton. I got your message. Is everything ok?"

"Hey baby! We don't know yet. There's still no word on what caused her brain to swell. The doctors are still running tests to find out what's going on."

"How are you holding up?" Milton inquired.

"I'm doing good. I know Big Mama, and she'll be fine."

"I hope so. If you need me, you make sure you call, ok?"

"I will do just that. Don't worry, everything will be fine. I don't know how long I'm gonna be here. I'll call and let you know."

"Take as much time as you need. When I start to miss you, you can bet that I'll make my way there to see you. Would you like that?"

"Yes, I would. Well, I need to go and freshen up, so I can get back to the hospital. I'll call you later tonight."

"Ok, my love. I'll pray for you and your family. I love you!"

"I love you too. I'll talk to you later tonight. Bye."

"Ok, bye."

I got out of the car and headed toward the side door. Marshall followed me with a big smile on his face.

"What are you smiling about?" I questioned.

"Nothing. Your new man?" Marshall asked.

"Yes."

"D, I'm so mad at you. Why haven't you told me about him?" Marshall said as he unlocked the door and walked into the house.

"Well, I wanted to make sure it was gonna work."

I felt bad because I talked to Marshall all the time, but I never mentioned that I was dating Milton. I usually kept him informed when I was dating someone. He was hurt. I could tell by the look on his face.

"Marshall, I'm sorry. I don't know why I didn't tell you."

"It's cool. You've been through a lot with your past relationships. I understand. But don't you ever do that again or I will kick your butt! Understood?"

"Understood, Sir."

"Knowing you, he's probably a lawyer or something of that nature." Marshall stated.

"As a matter of fact, he is a lawyer. He's a partner at the law firm where he works. I don't know what he sees in me." I said.

"D, stop it! Don't start with that insecurity crap again. I told you that you are a good catch for anyone. You need to believe in yourself more. I don't know what happened to you to make you start doubting yourself." Marshall scolded.

"I'm just kiddin." I said to stop the reprimand.

"When we were growing up, I always looked up to you. You were so self-assured and confident and I wanted to be just like you. Now, listen to yourself! You sound so defeated. Why?"

"Marshall, I was just joking. Chill out ok! Listen, I need to freshen up before we head back to the hospital. We can talk about this on the way there. K?" I said as I headed to the bathroom.

"Yeah, that's fine." Marshall responded.

I was in shock. I never knew Marshall looked up to me the way he did. I lost my confidence after my relationship with Winton ended. I was never the same after that incident. I was too consumed with bitterness and anger to allow myself the freedom to be confident.

I took a long sensual shower trying to wash away any doubt and uncertainty. I wanted to make sure I was fresh to face my parents and my brother. I knew Marshall would be waiting to pick up where we left off. I wasn't in the mood for a lecture.

"Marshall, I'm ready." I yelled from the bathroom.

Marshall lived in a nice three-bedroom two-story brick house with two and half baths. It was beautifully decorated

138

like something out of Country Living. My brother definitely had impeccable taste.

"Well, let's go, and don't think you're off the hook, either!" Marshall responded.

I entered the living room dressed in a black Nike Sweat Suit. Marshall was standing at the door looking at me with eyes that made me feel like a three-year-old. I immediately began to speak.

"Marshall, I'll be honest. I haven't been quite the same since Winton left me. I started doubting myself and didn't feel that I was worthy of love. I don't expect for you to understand, but life hasn't always been easy for me."

"No one ever said life would be easy, but I think it would have helped if you would have at least told me what was going on with you. You know I would have been there in a heartbeat."

"Well, I didn't think you would understand. Most heterosexual men are not exactly thrilled to converse about gay relationships."

"D, you're my brother. I have never cared about your sexuality. Did you think I didn't know what was going on in high school with you and Edwin?" Marshall asked.

I couldn't believe my ears. My mouth dropped open. I didn't think anyone knew about Edwin and me. We always tried to be secretive and not let on to our relationship. Needless to say, Marshall cracked my face. I tried to play it off.

"Marshall, what are you talking about?"

"D, do I look stupid? You heard what I said. I knew about you and Edwin as well as most other people."

"What do you mean?"

"Do you honestly think that no one could see the way both of you would light up when the other one was around? I sure noticed it. Most people were just afraid to say anything because Edwin was a jock."

I wasn't buying it for one second because if people suspected that Edwin and I were together rumors would have surely surfaced in that small town. They never did.

"Marshall, you're just making this stuff up. You know how people would gossip, and that would have been a big scandal. I could see the headlines now, High School Jock in Homosexual Love Affair."

"D, I remember the night that you and Edwin broke up. It was on the day you graduated from high school, and you two met at your usual hideout in the country."

I felt like a child who got caught with his hand in the cookie jar. If there were a hole in the floor, I certainly would have crawled through it.

"Since you seem to know so much, tell me what happened." I laughed nervously.

"I have a confession. I used to follow you all the time because I wanted to know why you were always so happy. I discovered the reason one night when I accidentally found your diary. You described in detail your affair with Edwin and the place where you two met at night. My curiosity got the best of me one night, so I decided to search for the hideout on Section 5. I found it. But before I could leave, you and Edwin showed up and that's when he told you that he didn't want to see you anymore because of his kid."

"You invaded my privacy." I said. "I can't believe you read my diary. How dare you!"

"D, I apologize for the intrusion, but you were my only friend. I got mad when I found out that you were seeing Edwin. I tried my best to break it up, but you never noticed."

"What do you mean you tried to break it up?" I questioned.

"I always wanted you to do something with me when you were getting ready to go meet Edwin. I knew he was a dog, and I didn't want you to be with him. I knew that bastard would hurt you, but I couldn't say anything because you would have found out that I knew about you being gay."

"I don't understand, Marshall."

"Well, Edwin was seeing this girl in one of my classes. She would talk about him all the time, so I knew he was messing around on you. I wanted to kick his ass, but you would have been upset."

"Thinking back now, I really wished you would have said something."

"It wasn't my place and besides you thought you were in love."

"I was really your only friend?" I asked purposely changing the subject.

"Yes, you are still one of the greatest people I know."

"I used to be, but now I'm only a fragment of the person I used to be."

"Ok, whatever! We will discuss these things in more detail before you leave. Right now, we need to go check on Big Mama." Marshall said as he headed out the door.

I followed him still in shock that he read my inner most personal thoughts. He came into my room the night Edwin broke up with me and wouldn't leave even after I chewed him out.

The more I thought about it, I realized that Marshall was very protective of me. He never would allow anyone to bother me although he was younger. I smiled just thinking about his kindness, but I began to feel sad thinking about how I took him for granted. I didn't include him in my life as much as I should have. I shut him out because of my anger and bitterness. I vowed that I would make it up to him.

We rode to the hospital in silence. Part of my brain thought about Big Mama and the other part thought about Marshall. Big Mama always told me that my brother was a gift from God. He truly was.

CHAPTER TWENTY - SEVEN

"Any changes with Big Mama?"

"No, she's still the same." My mother responded."

Marshall and I took a seat next to my mother. She looked very tired even more so than she did when I first arrived. My daddy was staring off in the distance.

"Mother, you look exhausted. Why don't you and Daddy go on home and rest for a bit? D and I will stay. We'll call you if there is any change." Marshall said.

"Levi, you ready to go? The boys will stay." My mother said.

"No, I don't need to rest. I'll be fine." My daddy said.

"Daddy, you look just as exhausted as Mother. Please go get some rest. I don't want to have to visit you here as well. D and I will take care of everything." Marshall stated.

"Daddy, I agree with Marshall. You should rest, and then you can come back." I responded.

"Alright" He shouted. "But if there are any changes, you make sure to call me. Ok?"

"Yes Sir." Marshall and I said in unison.

My daddy and his foolish pride. He always had to play the tough guy role, although it was obvious that he was worried sick. Since he was the eldest child, it was thought that his behavior stemmed from having to play the man of the house after the passing of his father.

My mother hugged Marshall and me as she headed to the elevator. My daddy slowly followed with his head hanging down. I wanted to reach out to him to let him know that Big Mama was going to be all right, but I decided against it. My thoughts wouldn't have been received very well.

As the elevator doors opened, my sister, Lisa stepped out into the lobby with her sunglasses on her face like she was a celebrity or something. My parents stood in front of the elevator frozen in their tracks. We were all in shock that my sister had the nerve to show up after turning her nose up to the family. My mother was the first to speak.

"Hello Lisa, I'm glad you could make it." My mother said with a strained voice.

"Hello, Mother. I'm here for Big Mama. Is it possible that I can see her?" Lisa asked, ignoring my father's presence.

"You can go in and sit with her, but she is still unconscious." Mother responded.

Lisa walked pass my mother's extended hand. My mother had a hurt look on her face, and my father stood there with a look of disgust on his. No one was happy that Lisa had shown up. We knew she would be up to her old tricks. I, however, was ready for battle. I had been waiting for an opportunity to put her in her place. I knew eventually she would slip up, and I would be waiting.

She walked over to where Marshall and I were standing. She rolled her eyes at me. I braced myself for what was about to come.

"Dae'Mon, I'm surprised you left faggotville to come visit Big Mama." Lisa said laughing.

"Excuse me!" I said.

"Lisa, what is your fucking problem?" Marshall asked harshly.

"Why is he here? We don't need his kind here upsetting the family." Lisa said looking at me with repugnance in her eyes.

"You little self-righteous bitch! I'm surprised you pulled your head out of your ass long enough to think about someone other than yourself. Are you that stupid? No one wants you here, so why don't you raise the fuck up out of here!" I yelled.

"I'm not going any where. Yo faggot ass is the one that needs to leave." Lisa screamed.

My parents ran over to the sitting area where we were standing. I could see the anger in their eyes.

"Lisa, that's enough! We're in a hospital. Please keep your voice down!" My mother said.

"I came here to see Big Mama, and this punk ass bitch verbally assaulted me." Lisa replied.

I rolled my eyes. I could feel my central nervous system shutting down. I was on a mission to shut her down for good.

"You ignorant ass ho! You the one falling up in here like you all that when you ain't shit, and you never gonna be shit! Bitch!"

"Dae'Mon, that's enough! She's not worth it!" Marshall said as he grabbed the small of my back.

"Please keep your voices down, this is a hospital!" The nurse said as she approached us. "If this continue, we will have to ask you all to leave." The nurse said as she walked away.

I was so embarrassed. Everyone in the ICU was staring at us. I wanted to haul off and bitch slap Lisa. I became even more enraged that my father just stood there and didn't say anything.

"Well, you should ask this AIDS infested mothafucker to leave!" Lisa said.

Mother drew back and slapped Lisa across her face. "How dare you embarrass us this way?" My mother screamed.

Lisa stood there in shock, rubbing the spot where my mother had smacked her. Tears streamed down her face. My mother grabbed her by the arm and led her to the elevator. My father followed slowly behind them as the doors opened, and they got on.

I took a seat on the couch in the waiting area. I put my hands over my face trying to hold back the tears. Marshall took a seat next to me and put his hand on my shoulder.

"Ooh, I hate that stupid bitch! Why did she have to show up?" I said as tears rolled down my face.

"Dae'Mon, please calm down! Lisa is stupid and not worth your energy. You can't let her get to you! If she comes back, I want you to ignore her. Promise me!" Marshall said.

"I'm not sure if I can Marshall. She said some cruel things about me. I just can't let that go." I responded.

"Well, you need to be the mature one. Like I said, she's not worth it. It's not our fault that her husband beats her ass. She's the fool to stay in that type of relationship. The hell with her!" Marshall said as he handed me a napkin from the box on the table in front of us.

"You're right. I'll just ignore her if she comes back." I said as I wiped my eyes with the napkin Marshall had given to me.

"That's good to hear. Now, let me see that beautiful smile of yours." Marshall said with a huge grin on his face.

I mustered up enough strength to give him a half smile. I was hurt and not in the smiling mood. As I laid back in the chair, I could see my father approaching us from the elevator.

"Hey guys, we're gonna head home now. Don't worry! We're taking Lisa with us. Your mother is going to talk with her. Dae'Mon, I'm sorry for the things your sister said. That was very mean of her." My father said as he turned and walked away.

I sat in my chair in shock. I couldn't believe my father uttered those words. I didn't think he cared about my feelings. I was wrong. Marshall appeared to be in shock as well. He sat there speechless. I was becoming overwrought with emotion, so I decided to get some fresh air. I stood up and headed to the elevator.

"Where are you going?" Marshall asked.

"I need some time alone. I'll be back." I said as I pushed the down button for the elevator.

"Just hurry back! I don't want to be here by myself."

I didn't respond as I got on the elevator. I pushed the button for the lobby. My mind was spinning in circles. I was hoping that Big Mama would soon get better so I could leave. The painful memories from my childhood began to resurface. I walked outside as tears streamed down my face again.

I found a bench located on the East Side of the building. I took a seat and buried my face in my hands and softly sobbed. I needed to release years of frustration, hurt and anger. I didn't want to go through another moment of feeling hopeless and worthless.

I felt a tap on my shoulder. I looked up with tear stained eyes to find my brother sitting next to me.

"D, what's wrong?" Marshall inquired.

"There's something in my eyes."

"D, I'm sorry for what Lisa said to you. She's bitter and angry, and she took her anger out on you, which was wrong of her. I apologize for her behavior."

"I'm not worried about Lisa. She's nothing to me." I said as the tears continued to flow.

"Then, why are you crying?" He asked.

"I was just thinking about when I lived here and all the stuff that I went through. I really don't think I have ever gotten over how Daddy treated me, nor have I gotten over what Edwin did to me all those years ago. It still hurts."

"I know it's not easy, but one thing you can do is to work on fixing your relationship with Daddy. The situation with Edwin can be addressed in only one way. I think you should confront him and tell him how he made you feel. That will start the healing process."

"I don't know, Marshall. Daddy is so stubborn, and I haven't seen Edwin in ten years. I'm not sure if that would be a good idea."

"Just think about what I said! It sure beats sitting around crying about it and allowing it to affect your relationship with Milton."

Marshall got up and walked away. He left me sitting there pondering my next move. I knew that I had to deal with my unresolved issues if I wanted to have a healthy, productive relationship with Milton.

I rose from my seat and gathered myself before I returned to the waiting room. Marshall was sitting with his eyes closed. He looked as if he was praying. I didn't want to disturb him, so I found a seat several feet from where he was sitting. He opened his eyes as I sat down.

"Have you made a decision yet?" Marshall asked.

"Yes, I have. I realize that I must put an end to the pain that I feel, so I'm going to talk with daddy, and if I see Edwin, I'll talk with him as well."

"I'm glad to hear that. I don't know if you realize it or not, but Edwin works at the college. He's an assistant football coach and a P. E. teacher.

My eyes bulged. I was surprised that Edwin would teach anything other than Heartbreak 101.

"You got to be kidding, right? He actually graduated from college?"

"Yes, he asks about you all the time."

"I hope you didn't tell him anything about me."

"I do. I remind him every chance I get as to how successful you are. I just want him to know what he let get away."

"You are so crazy, Marshall."

We laughed.

I saw a lady in a white hospital jacket approaching us out of the corner of my eye. I was praying it wasn't a doctor with any more bad news. Marshall and I rose to our feet.

"Hi, I'm Doctor Stewart. Are you with the Greene Family?" she asked.

"Yes, we are. We're her grandsons." Marshall responded.

"Ok, where is your father? He wanted me to keep him informed with your grandmother's condition."

"He went home to rest. We'll let him know what's going on." I said.

"Ok, well the swelling in Ms. Greene's brain has stopped which is good news. However, the fact that she is still unconscious has us concerned. The next 24 hours are very critical. We're keeping an around the clock eye on her. I'll let you know if there are any more changes." The doctor said as she turned and walked away.

Marshall and I just stood frozen. I was happy to hear that the swelling stopped. In my mind, that was a good sign. I felt that Big Mama was going to be ok, and it wouldn't be long before she would wake.

"D, do you think that's good news?" Marshall asked.

"Yes, I think it is. The swelling has stopped and I believe once everything returns to normal Big Mama will be just fine."

"I hope you're right. I'm so scared. I don't know what I would do without her. She has truly been my inspiration."

"Marshall, stop talking like that. Big Mama is going to be fine. Just wait, you'll see." I said as I hugged my brother.

Big Mama's condition would remain the same for the next three weeks. I kept in touch with Milton and the office. I did as much work as I could from Marshall's house. Milton kept me uplifted by calling to check on me and to say that he wanted to come down to be with me. I was against the idea. I didn't think my father was ready to meet Mr. Parker at the time.

Big Mama had always told me that the Lord may not come when you want him, but he would always be right on time. She couldn't have been more correct.

CHAPTER TWENTY - EIGHT

Big Mama opened her eyes for the first time in over a month. Her warm smile lit up the room. She was happy to see Marshall and me standing by her side. I was happy that she had come back to me. I never doubted she would.

She was very thirsty and wanted water to sooth her dry mouth. Marshall poured water into a cup and handed it to Big Mama. She didn't have much strength and almost dropped the cup into the bed. Marshall held the cup as she took a long drink.

"Thank you baby. Now, how are my favorite grandbabies doing?" Big Mama asked in her usual chipper tone.

"We're fine. How do you feel?" I asked.

"I'm a little tired but happy to be alive. I couldn't leave dis world without seeing yo new friend again." Big Mama stated.

"Big Mama, what are you talking about?" I inquired.

"Yeah, Big Mama. What are you saying?" Marshall said.

"Why you boys trying to fool yo old Big Mama. He come to the hospital to visit me. He a handsome feller."

Marshall and I looked at each other. I was perplexed, thinking that she was probably delusional since she had been unconscious for so long. No one had been to the hospital other than Marshall, Lisa, my parents and me.

"Big Mama, are you sure you're ok?" Marshall asked.

"Yeah Mama is fine. Dae, where is yo friend?"

Dae was the name Big Mama called me when I was growing up. Big Mama hadn't called me by that name in a long time. I knew something had to be wrong.

"Big Mama, what friend? No one has been here other than the family."

I felt that she was obviously speaking of someone else. I looked over what she said and excused myself from the room to call my parents.

"Hello…" My daddy said.

"Daddy, this is Dae'Mon." I responded.

"Is everything alright son?" He asked.

"Yes sir. I just wanted to call and let you know that Big Mama has awakened from the coma. She's just as lively as ever. I'll tell her that you and Ma are on the way."

"Ok son, we'll be there in a bit." He said as he hung up the phone.

I returned to Big Mama's room only to face more questions about this mysterious friend she supposedly met.

"Dae, go git yo handsome friend so I can talk to him agen." Big Mama said.

"Big Mama, I'm here alone. My friend is still in Kansas City, so you couldn't have met him."

"Baby, Mama know what she talkin bout. He jus as tall as you but got more meat on his bones. He some type of lawyar, ain't he baby?"

"Yes Ma'am, but how did you know that?" I asked with a quizzical look on my face.

"Ain't you listenin baby? I told you he come to see Big Mama."

"Ok, Big Mama. You need to get some rest before Ma and Daddy gets here. So, you rest and we'll be back in a little while. Ok?"

"Ok, Big Mama tired and I gonna rest. You bring that friend of yurs back to see me, you here?" Big Mama said while shaking her finger at me.

"Yes Ma'am. I said as I leaned over to kiss her forehead. "Big Mama, Lisa is here also to visit you. Are you ok with that?" I asked.

"Yeah baby! I want to see my grandbaby, no matter how silly she is. Big Mama can handle her, so don't you worry." Big Mama said as she laid back on the pillow.

Marshall and I left the room. I was at a lost for words. There was no way Big Mama could have known about Milton. I never told her about him. I was in a daze.

"D, what you thinking about?" Marshall asked.

"How Big Mama knew about Milton. I mean I never spoke to her about him. When I would go in and sit with her. I'd never mentioned him. It amazes me that she keeps asking for someone that she has never met. I'm confused. I know Milton is not here. He couldn't be. I just spoke to him this morning, and he was at home in Kansas City."

"I wouldn't worry about it. Big Mama has been out for so long, she probably doesn't know what she's saying."

"Yeah, you're right. I'll drop it for now. I need to call Milton anyway. Excuse me I'll be right back."

I took a walk outside to call Milton. I wanted to tell him the good news about Big Mama. When I called, I didn't receive an answer. Where could he be? I dialed his cell phone and his voice mail came on. I was getting worried. Milton hadn't mentioned anything to me about going anywhere. I left a message and told him to call me as soon as he returned.

I returned to the waiting room where my mother and father had now joined Marshall. Everyone was so happy and rejuvenated. I was happy to finally see them smile especially since they looked so run down when I first arrived a month earlier. I didn't see any signs of Lisa so I thought she had gone back to Jackson until I heard a voice behind me. I slowly turned around.

"Dae'Mon, I just want to apologize for the things I said to you earlier. I'm just going through some things, and I don't know what came over me." Lisa said.

"Just forget about it! I have." I replied.

"I feel just terrible for the things that I said."

"It's not important to me anymore, Lisa. I realized a long time ago that I don't need anyone to validate my existence, unlike you!" I said harshly.

I walked away feeling proud that I let her know that her existence didn't mean anything to me. She stood there dumbfounded. I joined Marshall who was engaged in conversation with my parents.

"Hey, you two. Have you gone in to see Big Mama?" I asked.

"No, we were just about to go in when you walked up." My mother said.

"Ok, I think she's still not 100% because she kept talking about meeting a friend of mine from Kansas City. I don't know what she's talking about."

"We'll find out when we get in there." My father responded.

They headed off to Big Mama's room with Lisa following behind them, as Marshall and I stayed in the waiting room. We took a seat and were engaged in lively chit chatter when I heard someone call my name. The voice sounded very familiar, but I knew my ears were deceiving me. I turned around and to my surprise, Milton was standing just a few feet away from where Marshall and I were sitting.

I leaped from my chair and ran over to him. I gave him a big hug, almost knocking him backwards. I wanted to kiss him, but I refrained due to the surroundings. Milton had a huge smile on his face.

"Milton, what are you doing here? I told you I would be fine and not to come." I said although I was very happy to see him.

"I know what you said, but I was not about to miss my baby's birthday."

I was so consumed with Big Mama's health that I had forgotten all about my birthday. What a wonderful surprise? I was completely in shock.

"Milton, you are too good to me. What would I do without you?"

"Ahem…" Marshall said clearing his throat to get my attention.

"Oh, I'm so sorry. Milton, this is my brother Marshall."

"Oh my God, there are two of you." Milton said as he extended his hand to Marshall. "It's good to finally meet you." Milton said.

"It's nice to finally meet you. I've heard a lot about you from D." Marshall said.

"All good I hope." Milton responded.

We laughed.

"Of course, it was all good. It's weird that you're here because my grandmother was just talking about meeting my lawyer friend. But how did she know you were coming?" I said.

"This is weird. A scene from the Twilight Zone." Marshall said laughing.

"Well, I stopped by to see her. I wanted to meet the great Ms. Greene, so I could seek her permission to marry you."

"Whatever!" I said laughing.

"I'm telling the truth. But you don't have to believe me." Milton replied.

"Doesn't matter! I'm just happy that you're here with me."

I got a little too excited seeing him. I wanted to jump his bones in the middle of the hospital lobby. It had been over a month since I had seen my man, and I was getting aroused with him there before my eyes.

"Marshall, if you will excuse us? I need to speak to Milton in private." I said.

"Oh, I understand." Marshall said with a big smile on his face.

Milton and I sneaked into an unoccupied room. We close the door and began to passionately kiss. We hungered for each other's touch. I wanted to take him right there in the vacant room but was too afraid that we would get caught.

We regained our composure and headed back to the waiting room. Marshall was smiling as we approached him. It was almost as if he knew what we had been doing. I wasn't concerned because I had my man with me and my grandmother was conscious. I couldn't have been happier.

My happiness was shattered by the thought of my father meeting Milton. I had to ask myself if I was ready to face the music.

Hum!...

CHAPTER TWENTY - NINE

Big Mama was released from the hospital a few days after regaining consciousness. Her health had returned to normal even though the doctors were never able to figure out what caused the problem.

All was well. My family seemed to have been enjoying Milton's company including my father. I was surprised because my daddy had never met any of my male friends before, so I thought he would explode. He never did. In fact, he and Milton engaged in friendly conversation. I felt that my daddy's behavior resulted from the scare of almost losing Big Mama. I was more than thrilled that he accepted Milton as my lover.

Lisa returned to Jackson on the day Big Mama was released from the hospital. We didn't speak another word to each other after the day I read her at the hospital. Marshall overheard her telling my mother that she really screwed up when she insulted me. My mother told her that she should think next time before she speaks. My sentiments exactly!

Milton and I stayed a few extra days to ensure Big Mama was going to be ok. She assured us both that she was fine, and we could return to Kansas City. As much as we wanted to be alone, we knew that Big Mama really didn't want us to leave. She adored Milton and told me that I was lucky to have someone like him in my life.

I was truly happy for the first time in a long time. I spoke with Edwin while I was there and talked to him about how he made me feel the night he ended our relationship. He acknowledged that he was just dumb, immature and really didn't know what he wanted. I was happy that I was able to put that bad memory behind me.

My father and I took some time to reflect on our relationship and what could be done to enhance it. He talked openly about his feelings toward homosexuality and made a promise that he would try to get a better understanding of it to ensure that we continue to build on a solid father and son relationship.

It was amazing that it took Big Mama's near death experience to bring about a change in our lives. I was a different person after that ordeal. I was a changed person, a better person. I could also see the change in my father. A miracle in disguise.

I became overwrought with tears the night before Milton and I was scheduled to fly back to Kansas City. I was having such a wonderful time with my family that I didn't want to leave, but I knew my life was in Kansas City with Milton.

Milton and I flew back to Kansas City promising that we would return for a visit during the Christmas holidays.

—

"Edwin, it is good to see you. You're still looking good."

"Oh Dae'Mon, I'm so glad to see you." He said as he gave me a hug. "I have never stopped thinking about you. I was always wondering what you were doing."

"I've been doing great. I have a very good life in Kansas City, and I'm very happy."

"That's good. Man, you look good. How long are you in town?"

"For a few more days. Big Mama is doing much better now, so it's time for me to head home."

"I was hoping that I would get to spend some time with you before you left. I guess that's out of the question."

"You're spending time with me now."

"No, I was hoping that we could have dinner and reminisce about old times."

"Why in the hell would I want to reminisce about the past?"

"Dae'Mon, I don't understand the anger. Did I say something wrong?"

I laughed. "You're joking right? You have to be fucking joking! Edwin, do you recall graduation night? Do you remember the things that you said to me?" I questioned.

"Somewhat, but most of that stuff I have forgotten about."

"Well, I just want you to know that I still remember as if it were yesterday. You said some cruel things to me. You tore me down, and I'm still suffering somewhat to this day."

"Dae'Mon, you have to let those things go."

"Oh really! You were the one who mistreated me Edwin. I loved you, and I thought you felt the same. Obviously I was wrong. But, I'm here to tell you that I'm a stronger person today because of you. I have a good man that loves me and that's all that matters. It took me years to build up enough courage to tell you how I felt. I will not allow you to hurt me anymore."

"Dae'Mon, I was young and stupid. It wasn't until after you left that I realized that I was in love with you. I wanted to come to you, but I couldn't. I thought you must have hated me for the way I treated you. I apologize from the bottom of my heart and I ask for your forgiveness. I never meant to hurt you."

"Well Edwin, I forgive you. But a love like mine, you will never know again." I said.

"You're right Dae'Mon. You were too good for me. I regret that I didn't appreciate your love back then cuz I haven't been successful in relationships since. No one I meet even comes close to loving me the way you did. Damn, I was such a fool to let you get away, but I'm glad that you're happy. I wish you the best, and I will always love you." Edwin said as he gave me a hug.

I felt as if a heavy burden had been lifted from my shoulders. The past was finally behind me once and for all.

—

"Son, I just don't understand all of this homosexuality crap. It just ain't natural in the eyes of the Lord."

"Daddy, I don't understand it myself, but I can tell you that this is who I am. I can't change the way I was born."

"So, you think you were born this way?"

"Yes Sir, I do. For as far back as I can remember, I knew there was something different about me. I didn't know what it was at the time, but I knew that I had a strong attraction to the boys in the neighborhood. That is something that I didn't learn from anyone because there were no other gay people around that I knew of, so it was something that was embedded in me since birth."

"Son, the Bible says that it's an abomination. It's a sin."

"We all have sinned and come short of the glory of God. No one is perfect Daddy. However, God made me in his own image, and he didn't make a mistake. He knew that I was going to be gay before I was born. One thing I want you to remember is that the Bible was told orally for years before it was ever written. Then, it was translated to English from a different language. Whose to say that the people who wrote it or the people who translated it, did not change it to suit their own needs?"

"Now, you're talking that college mumbo. They have clouded your head."

"No, your head seems to be clouded because you have closed your mind to trying to get a good understanding of who I am. I'm not looking for your acceptance. All I ask is that you respect me just as I respect you."

"I've never disrespected you Dae'Mon." My daddy said defensively.

"Yes you have. You were not fair to me when I was growing up. You treated me like I was a leper or something worse. You made me feel as if you didn't want me around."

"Son, I didn't want you growing up to be a sissy. That's why I was tough on you. I wanted you to be a man."

"Daddy, just because I am gay doesn't make me any less of a man. The only difference is who I choose to love. My relationship with men is no different from a relationship between a man and a woman. You can't change who I am."

"Son, I just don't want you to go through life struggling and getting that AIDS crap."

"Daddy, I have a very comfortable life in Kansas City, and you would know that if you came to visit. I think you would be proud of how I turned out and all that I have accomplished. One more thing! That "AIDS crap" that you mentioned affects everyone, not just gay people."

"Dae'Mon, I don't know if I can accept this. It just ain't right."

'Daddy, I never asked for your acceptance. Like I said before, I just want you to give my partner and I the same amount of respect that I give to you. I'm not one to flaunt my sexuality in anyone's face, so you don't have to worry about that. I'm not going to bring embarrassment and shame to the family if that's what you're worried about."

"Dae'Mon, I don't know. It's all so confusing."

"Yeah I know. I'm confused as well about a lot of things, but that has not caused me to close my mind to the possibility of exploring further. Daddy, you and I have never had a close relationship, and I don't want one of us to be on our deathbed before we realize that we have wasted valuable time worrying about something so insignificant."

"You're right son. I tell you what I'm going to do. I will do a better job at trying to understand who you are. It doesn't mean I will accept your homosexuality, but I will at least attempt to get a better understanding of it."

"That's all I ask. I can help you. I can send you books and send you information on groups that specialize in this type of thing."

"Ok, Dae'Mon. I will do this before it's too late. I know I have never told you this before, but I'm very proud of you. And I love you son."

I was in shock because my father had never said he loved me before.

"I love you too daddy." I said as I hugged him for the first time in my life.

CHAPTER THIRTY

The return trip to Kansas City was uneventful. Milton and I slept during the entire plane ride. Cold weather and dark clouds greeted us when the plane landed at the airport. I became gloomy thinking about all that I hadn't taken care of during my stay in Mississippi. I had neglected my responsibilities such as paying bills, cleaning, etc. I thought I would have a pile of mail just waiting for me to open, and a foul odor that would run me underground. I was pleasantly surprised when I opened the door to my loft to find it exceptionally clean and no mountain of paper waiting on me.

I had a puzzled look on my face.

"Milton, what gives?" I asked as I stepped inside.

"What do you mean?" Milton said as he locked the door.

I stood in one spot taking in my loft as if I hadn't been there before.

"Where is my mail? And did you clean my apartment?"

"Your mail is on the dining room table, and yes I had a cleaning service to come and keep the apartment neat and tidy while you were away."

"You are too good to me." I said as I walked over to Milton and gave him a big hug.

"Well, I felt that you had enough to worry about. I didn't want you to come back and have to lift a finger to do anything." He said as he released me from his embrace.

"Well that was very sweet of you. I'm surprised the utilities companies haven't turned off my services."

Milton laughed as he made his way over to the sofa.

"Milton Parker, what have you done?"

"Baby, I just paid the bills. I didn't want you to worry about it when you got back."

"Milton, you shouldn't have. I should have known you were up to something when you kept asking questions about my services. I'll punish you later."

"Since I'm going to be punished, I better confess to something else that I did."

I placed my hands on my hips and rolled my eyes toward the ceiling.

"What did you do?"

Milton began to stare at his hands as he began to speak.

"Baby, you forgot that your lease expires at the end of this month, and your landlord came by one day when I was here. He asked if you were going to stay, and I told him no."

He put his head down just waiting for me to go off. It was fun to see him sweat.

"Milton, I really wish you had discussed this matter with me before you made a decision. We just talked about that not too long ago, but you didn't listen. You shall be punished for that as well. Now, I guess I have no other choice but to move into the condo with you."

A big smile grew on his face. He looked like a little kid who had just arrived at Disney World for the first time.

"Well, I was hoping you would. Dae'Mon, I promise I'll do right by you. Please say yes!" He pleaded.

"I'll have to think about it. I'll get back to you in a week." I stated.

"Well, actually sweetheart, you have to be out in two days. Today is the 29th."

"Oh my God, you're right. Well, since you wanted to be grown and handle everything. You need to decide where to put my things. Also, I need a closet for my clothes and shoes. I want everything taken care of by tomorrow."

"Ok, no problem. It's already done." He said with a huge grin on his face.

"Run that by me one more time?"

"Baby, I didn't know when you were coming back, and I figured that you would say that. So I have the movers coming tomorrow. They will take your things to storage until you decide what you want to do with them."

"You little sneak." I said laughing. "I'm going to spank you." I said as I ran after him as he jumped up and ran into the bedroom.

I followed him, and he received his punishment. We made love for the first time in over a month. I felt like an erupting volcano. Lava just flowing and flowing.

—

I moved into the condo with a very elated Milton. He was bouncing off the walls like he was on speed or something. He cooked for me and catered to all of my needs. I had become spoiled, but I knew I had to put an end to it because if I didn't I would come to expect it all the time. I knew Milton couldn't keep behaving in this manner.

We settled down and became comfortable living together. I had to rearrange some of the furnishing to my satisfaction. He didn't say a word as I went through putting my touch on the condo.

I hesitatingly returned to work. The time I spent in Mississippi gave me an opportunity to reflect on my life. I realized that I wasn't' happy at my job, and it was best for me to leave. Of course, Milton was very supportive.

"Dae'Mon, you can quit if you like. I got all the bills covered, so you don't have to worry about that." He stated.

As good as the offer sounded, I wasn't going to stay home like I was a housewife with nothing to do but have lunch with my girlfriends. No thank you! I decided that I would stay on until the end of the year and would then submit my resignation.

That wasn't the answer that Milton wanted to hear. I was raised to be independent, and I was not about to stay home and allow my man to take care of me.

I had enough money in the bank to allow me not to work for nine months to a year before I had to find employment. You forgot I obtained a degree in Economics. I knew how to invest and save which I started soon after graduating from college. Besides, I wouldn't have known what to do with myself sitting at home all day.

I continued to work as the weather grew colder. Fall had turned into winter. As the seasons changed, my life changed again.

CHAPTER THIRTY - ONE

A heavy snowstorm blew through the city, leaving 8 inches of snow behind. It was bitterly cold and not advisable to be out in the weather unless it was absolutely necessary. I took heed to the warning. I stayed indoors.

Milton on the other hand had a meeting scheduled with a client that day in St. Joe. I didn't want him to go. I put up a fierce argument to keep him home but to no avail.

"The weather doesn't stop the court system, Dae'Mon."

I didn't care about the court system. The court system wouldn't care about me if he were killed in a car accident. I wanted my man home, but he wasn't hearing it. I tried another approach that also failed. I gave him the silent treatment.

"Oh, so you're not talking to me! That's fine. I'll find someone else to talk to while I'm out." Milton said.

"Cool, he can have your crazy ass!" I retorted as I walked off in a tizzy.

"So, you're talking to me now? Dae'Mon, don't be that way. I was only kidding. Don't be like that baby." He said as walked in the kitchen where I was standing.

I had my back to him. He put his arms around my waist and began to kiss my neck. I felt sparks trickling down my spine, but I wasn't going to give in to him this time. I was mad and wanted my way.

"No, leave me alone. I'm sure you can meet someone else to kiss. Besides, it's not going to work this time."

"We'll just see about that." Milton said as he spun me around to face him.

He planted a deep kiss on my soft lips. I didn't resist. Before I knew it, we were making love on the kitchen floor.

"Damn baby, that was so good, but I know what you're doing, Dae'Mon. It's not going to work." Milton said as we laid in the floor recovering.

"What?" I said playing dumb.

"You tried to work it on me, so I won't go out to visit my client. Baby, I promise you I will be fine. It's not like this is the first time I've driven in this stuff."

"I know it's not, but you weren't my man then. Milton, I'm just scared all right! I can't stand the thought of something happening to you. Please stay." I begged.

Milton got up from the floor and walked upstairs to the bedroom. I quickly jumped up and followed him. I was trying everything in my power to get him to stay home with me.

"Dae'Mon, I have to go visit my client. Please baby, I need you to understand."

"Yeah, I understand alright. You just don't care about my feelings." I responded harshly.

"That's enough, Dae'Mon!" Milton said sternly. "There should be no doubt in your mind about how much I love you. I don't want to ever hear you say that again. Do I make myself clear?"

"Yes…Yes, you do." I said as I took a seat on the edge of the bed.

"Alright! Now, I'm going to get dressed to make my meeting, and I will come home as soon as it's over. This meeting will last about an hour, and I should be home shortly afterwards. Don't worry, I'll be fine."

Milton walked over and took a seat next to me. He gently kissed my lips as he massaged my back. I felt myself being reeled in.

"Baby, please be careful. I want you back in one piece." I said.

"You've got a deal. I'll make dinner tonight."

Milton removed himself from the bed and walked into the bathroom to take a shower. I could hear the sound of the water running. I pondered how I would entertain myself while Milton was gone. I decided to call Justice.

"Hello." The voice said.

"May I please speak with Ms. Justice?"

"This is she. How are you Dae'Mon?"

"I'm just peachy. How are you?"

"Good, I'm getting ready to head out to meet my man."

"Oh I see. Why are you going out in this weather?"

"Because honey, my man is waiting to see me. Where is your other half?"

"Getting ready to go meet a client. I begged him not to go out in this weather, but he won't listen."

"Child, you need to get over it. The roads are not that bad. I've been out already. It's no worse than normal."

I rolled my eyes and laid back on the bed. This was not the support I was seeking from Justice. I wanted her to agree with me.

"But Justice…"

"But nothing! You need to stop acting like a child and let that man go do his job. He'll be back and then you can play house which I'm sure that's what you want to do anyway." Justice said laughing.

"I will have you to know Miss Missy that we played house already."

We laughed.

"You so crazy. We need to schedule a time to hook up, so you can meet my new beau, Howard."

"Oh! I'm free when you are. I'm sure I can fit you into my schedule, but make sure you call my secretary first."

We laughed.

"I heard she got fired from the sperm bank for drinking on the job."

Justice dropped the phone from laughing so hard.

"Girl, you are a fool." I said laughing.

"What's so funny?" Milton asked as he walked out of the bathroom.

"I'm talking to Justice." I responded. "Justice, you alright girl."

"Yeah, I'm fine. I can't breathe." She said as she started laughing all over again.

I started laughing as well all the while watching Milton prance around the room in his birthday suit. I could feel my temperature rising. I thought about attacking him but decided against it. I didn't' want him to think that I was trying to keep him from going to his meeting.

"Ok, I better go now." Justice said.

"Good. So what time are you going to meet Howard?"

"I'm about to leave in a few minutes. He wants to take me shopping and then have lunch in Westport."

"That sounds like fun. You could bring him by here since you're going to be in my neck of the woods."

"I'll ask him about it. I'm sure he won't mind."

"Good, I can't wait to meet him."

"Well, I have to run now my love. I'll call you to let you know what time we'll stop by."

"Ok, you be careful out there."

"I will. Tell Milton I said hello and I'll talk with you later."

"Ok, Ciao." I said as I hung up the phone.

I placed the phone back on the desk. I continued to watch Milton get dressed. He was an incredibly beautiful man.

"Like what you see?" He asked.

"I don't see anything." I retorted.

"You didn't say that a while ago when I was rocking your world." Milton said as he did the hand in the air snap.

We laughed.

"I don't know what you're talking about."

"Sure you don't. Oh Milton! Yes Milton! Yes! Yes." He said in his best imitation of me.

I threw a pillow at him. He moved as the pillow hit the wall.

"Touché'." He said laughing.

"Whatever."

Milton finally finished dressing. He looked so handsome in his Georgio Armani suit. Milton could make a burlap sack look good on his body.

"Ok baby. I'm about to go. Give me some love before I leave."

I removed myself from the bed and planted a passionate kiss on Milton's juicy lips. I was afraid to touch him in fear of wrinkling his suit.

"You be careful." I said as I gave him one last peck.

"I will. I love you!" Milton said.

"I love you too."

Milton walked out of the bedroom to leave for his meeting. I heard the living room door open and close. I was now alone.

I walked into the bathroom and turned the water on. I showered and then jumped back in bed. I laid there staring at the ceiling just thinking about my life. I was truly happy.

I was so deep in thought that I didn't hear the phone when it first rang.

"Hello." I answered.

"Dae'Mon. This is Milton. I just wanted to say thank you for loving me. You mean the world to me, and I love you so much."

"I know you do silly, and I love you too. You just make sure you hurry home."

"I will and Dae'Mon."

"Yes?" I said.

"I…" Milton paused.

"What is it baby?"

"I need to tell you something, and I'm not sure how you're going to react."

I could hear sadness in his voice. I became concerned. I wondered what he could possibly have to tell me that I didn't already know.

"What is it baby? Tell me. Are you alright?"

"Yes, I'm fine. I will tell you when I get home. Promise me you won't worry."

I sat up in the bed wondering what he wanted to tell me. I was confused, puzzled, dazed, you name it...

"Milton, you have me worried. Please tell me now."

"It's best that I talk to you in person. Dae'Mon, please believe that I love you."

"Milton, I know you do, so you can stop saying that. I want you to tell me what's on your mind. We shouldn't have secrets."

"I'll explain everything when I get home. Ok?"

"Ok, but you better be ready to talk or there is going to be a big price to pay. Understood?"

"Understood. I love you." Milton said sadly.

"I love you too! Stop sounding so sad. You sound like you're going to a funeral."

I could hear Milton disarming the car alarm. I wanted to run to the parking garage and force him to talk to me, but I wasn't dressed. I still had on my birthday suit.

"That's a possibility. I don't know what's going to happen when I tell you what I have to say."

"Milton Parker, you stop this right now. If you're not going to tell me, then you best to stop talking about it right now." I said sternly.

"Ok, I'll tell you. I'm pregnant."

"What?"

"I'm pregnant." Milton said as he burst into laughter.

"That's what you had to tell me?" I questioned.

"Yes, I just wanted to make you laugh."

"Well, the joke is going to be on you when you get home. I'm kicking you butt. I can't believe you did this to me. I'm a nervous wreck. I thought something was wrong with you. You're in trouble, mister!"

"I love you." Milton said.

I hung up the phone without responding. I couldn't find any words to say. In the words of that silly Agnes, "I'm just flabbergasting." I couldn't' do anything other than laugh. Milton pulled a fast one on me. However, I wouldn't be laughing for long.

CHAPTER THIRTY - TWO

I began to pace back and forth. It was the middle of the afternoon, and I had not heard from Milton. He left home at 9:30 earlier that morning. I became concerned. All sorts of things were going through my mind. I feared he had been involved in an accident and couldn't call to let me know. I feared he was spending time with someone else. I had to pull myself together. I was going crazy.

I couldn't take it anymore, so I decided to call him on his cell phone. I dialed the number and his voice mail came on. I hung up without leaving a message. I was puzzled because Milton always had his phone on. I really began to worry. I wanted to run out and search for him, but I didn't have a clue as to the first place to look.

My fears were temporarily alleviated when the phone rang. I smiled thinking it would be Milton.

"Hello." I said as I placed the phone next to my ear.

"Hey baby boy! What are you doing?" Justice asked.

"Waiting for that man of mine to come home. I'm worried because he said was only going to be gone an hour. It's 2:30 now, and he should have been back by now." I said as I took a seat on the edge of the bed.

"Dae'Mon, pull yourself together. You sound terrible. I'm sure Milton is fine."

"That's easy for you to say because your man is with you. I called his cell phone, and he didn't answer. That's not like him."

"Howard and I are gonna come over to keep you company, so you won't worry so much."

"Hold on! The other line is beeping."

"See that's probably him. Ok, I'll hold."

I pressed the flash button as the phone transferred to the second line.

"Hello."

"Yes, May I speak with Mr. Dae'Mon Greene?" the voiced asked.

"Yes this is Dae'Mon. May I ask who's calling?"

"Yes, this is Dr. Wright from North Kansas City Hospital."

My stomach began to churn. My worse fears were becoming a reality. I had to brace myself for what he was about to say.

"Yes Dr. Wright, what can I do for you?" I inquired.

"Well sir, Milton Parker asked me to call you to let you know that he has been admitted to the hospital. He was involved in a car accident."

I dropped the phone. I couldn't breathe. I felt as if the room was closing in on me. Panic sat in. I could hear a noise coming from the phone. It sounded as if Dr. Wright was trying to get my attention. After a brief moment, I regained my composure and went back to the phone.

"Dr. Wright, is Milton ok?" I asked hysterically.

"Yes, just a few minor cuts and scraps but nonetheless ok."

"Thank you Lord." I screamed out.

"We want to keep him overnight for observation, just to make sure he's ok. However, you will need to come here to pick him up. He's going to be very sore and not able to drive."

"Where is he?"

"He's in room 312."

"Thank you Dr. Wright. I'll be there shortly."

I hung up the phone without thinking. I was in such a panic that I forgot Justice was holding on the other line. The phone rang back which terrified me even more.

"Hello." I said as tears streamed down my face.

"Bitch! Don't you ever hang up on me again!" Justice said laughing.

"Justice, I'm so sorry." I whimpered.

"Dae'Mon, what's wrong? Why are you crying?"

"Milton has been in a car accident. He's at North Kansas City Hospital."

"Oh my God! Is he ok?" Justice asked hysterically.

"Yes. The doctor said he has a few cuts, but he's all right."

"Thank goodness. Why are you so upset?"

"Because Justice, I'm scared. I almost lost my baby."

"Dae'Mon, don't you think you're being just a tad bit dramatic?" Justice questioned.

"I wouldn't expect for you to understand how I feel. I gotta go to the hospital to see him."

"Would you like for Howard and I to take you?"

"No, I'm gonna be fine. You two enjoy the rest of the day."

"Dae'Mon, I don't think you should be driving in the state that you're in."

"No, I'm going to give Milton a mouth full. I told him not to take his ass out there, but he didn't' listen. Now look what has happened!" I said nastily.

"Dae'Mon Greene, you stop this foolishness! You will do no such thing. He is hurt and banged up enough, so don't you go there adding to it. I can't believe you. One minute you're crying and scared and the next minute you're plotting revenge. Stop acting so immature!" Justice scolded.

"You're right. I'll be on my best behavior. I need to get dressed, so I can go. I'll call you later."

"Dae'Mon, don't you take your ass to that hospital acting up. I mean it! Please be careful out there! Ok?"

"I'm fine, Justice. Don't worry!"

"Ok, call me later."

Ok, I will. Bye." I said as I hung up the phone.

I quickly got dressed and dashed out the door. I was still going to give Milton a piece of my mind. I didn't care what Justice said. I told him not to leave, but he didn't listen and ended up getting into an accident. He was in big trouble.

I made it to the hospital in 20 minutes. I realized that I was not thinking straight because I was speeding with ice on the roads. I was grateful that I made it in one piece. I ran into the hospital to find Milton lying in bed. He looked so pitiful. Before I could say anything, Milton spoke.

"Baby, go ahead and cuss me out."

"Now, why would I do that? What type of monster do you think I am?"

Yeah, yeah. I know, I know...Yes I said I was going to let him have it. I couldn't. My baby was hurt, and I couldn't bear to see him in that manner.

"Because you told me not to go out."

"Well the important thing is that you're ok. How do you feel?" I asked.

Milton had a bandage on his face and a few on his arms. He didn't appear to be in pain. I think his pride was hurt more so than anything else, simply because I told him not to go to that meeting.

"I'm fine. I'm just ready to go home."

"You'll be there soon, baby. Now, tell me what happened."

"Well, I was on my way home and stopped at a red light when this car just came out of nowhere and slid into me. He was seriously injured and tore his car to bits. It didn't do much damage to my car, just a few scratches. I'm thankful for that."

"Milton Parker. You could have been seriously hurt or even killed, and you're lying there being thankful that your car is not damaged. You better get a clue!" I scolded.

"I'm sorry baby. I was just saying that it could have been worse than it was."

"Well, you keep it up and you're going to be worse because I'm going to do some damage to you."

We laughed.

"Baby, I'm sorry for putting you through this. I know you were worried about me and I should have listened to you. Can you ever forgive me?" Milton asked.

"Yes, I forgive you, but there is always a price to pay." I laughed.

"Yeah, I'm indebted to you for life. What do you want?"

"No, I'm just teasing. You have given me all I need, and that's your love. That's all I want. Everything else is secondary. I'm just happy that you're ok."

"You are too good for me. I don't deserve you Dae'Mon." Milton said as tears rolled down his face.

I took a Kleenex from the box on the nightstand and wiped his face. I was puzzled as to why he was crying. I sat on the bed next to him.

"Milton, what's wrong? Why are you crying?" I inquired as I gently caressed his face.

"It's just I don't deserve you. Dae'Mon, I never meant to hurt you."

"Milton, what are you talking about? You haven't hurt me!"

Milton rolled onto his side with his back to me. He was acting strange, and I didn't know what was causing it. I thought that he was playing another one of his games again.

"Milton, is this another one of your tricks?" I questioned.

"No, it isn't. I'm serious this time, and I know you're going to leave me." He whined.

"Milton, what are you talking about? Why would I leave you?" I said sternly.

"I know you're going to hate me and probably want to kill me."

I grabbed him by his shoulder and turned him over onto his back. I looked him directly in his eyes.

"Milton, for the last time. Tell me what the hell you're talking about! I'm confused."

"I can't because you're gonna get mad."

I stood up from the bed and glared down at him. I was getting angry because he was playing games with me.

"I'm three days past mad. Stop playing games and tell me what is wrong!"

Tears rolled down his face. He began to tremble and shake as if something was wrong with him. I momentarily panicked.

"Milton, what's wrong? Why are you shaking? Do you want me to get the doctor?" I asked.

"No, I'm fine. I'm just sorry for hurting you."

I sighed and rolled my eyes toward the ceiling. I walked over to the window and looked out into the distance. I needed something to divert my attention from the situation at hand. I was angry beyond a doubt.

"Milton, I'm not going to ask you anymore what the problem is because I realize that you're not going to tell me. However, I'm letting you know right now that once you get home, we are going to have a serious discussion. If you can't tell me what's wrong, then I don't think we should be together anymore. Do I make myself clear?"

"Yes, but Dae'Mon, please don't say that. I love you, and I want to spend the rest of my life with you."

"Love doesn't have a thing to do with you not telling me what's wrong. I'm hurt and confused that you can't trust me enough to tell me why you're in so much pain. We've been together for almost a year now, and I really thought we were beyond this stage, but obviously not!" I said as I grabbed my coat.

"Dae'Mon, where are you going?" Milton asked.

"I'm leaving. You need some time alone to think about what I said. I'll come back tomorrow morning to get you. Please don't call me because I really don't want to talk to you anymore this evening! I'm very upset with you." I said as I walked out the door.

I could hear Milton calling for me, but I kept walking. I had to get away from the hospital to clear my head. I was bothered by the fact that he threw something out to me and didn't tell me what he was talking about. That was inexcusable.

I drove home in silence. My mind was wondering again and thinking all sorts of wild and weird things. I thought about turning around, so I could give Milton a piece of my mind. However, I decided that I would let him rest and think about our discussion.

I had no idea I was in for such a shock…

CHAPTER THIRTY - THREE

Milton's physical appearance horrified me when I arrived at the hospital to take him home. He looked as if he hadn't slept in days. I had never seen him look so tired and beat down. He was always so happy. I figured that the discussion that we were gonna have weighed heavily on his mind.

He was already dressed sitting on the bed with his head hanging down. It brought tears to my eyes to see him look so pitiful. I sat beside him and massaged his shoulders. He was very tensed and rigid. He didn't' move as I touched him. I tried to bring him out of his funk by kissing him on the lips. He didn't respond. I stood up and grabbed his hand. He sat there not moving. I pulled him up to me, and he kept his head down not looking directly at me.

"Milton, baby what's wrong?" I asked.

He didn't respond. He shook his head indicating that he was fine. I wasn't buying it. I knew something was wrong with my baby. I was going to get to the bottom of it even it took every ounce of strength I had.

"Milton, baby are you ok? Why won't you speak to me?" I said as I caressed his face.

"Dae'Mon, I'm so sorry." Milton said as he began to sob uncontrollably.

I grabbed him and held him in my arms. Tears were flowing down my face. I hated to see Milton in so much pain. I felt powerless because I felt there wasn't anything I could to do make him feel better.

"Baby, I love you and no matter what we will get through together." I said as I continued to hold him.

He continued to cry in my arms. The car accident really did a number on him. He had never been so emotional before. He was always so confident and self- assured, always in control.

179

"Milton, please stop crying so I can take you home. Please baby, you're making me scared. I love you so much, baby. I'm not going to leave you, please believe that! Are you gonna stop crying so we can leave?" I asked while wiping away his tears.

He shook his head in acknowledgement. He wiped his face with the napkin that I had given him, and followed me to the car without saying a word. The ride home was also filled with silence. Not once did he ever look in my direction. I was out of ideas and decided to wait for him to make the first move.

It was a bit of the same when we arrived home. He walked around like a zombie. I was getting upset so I decided to go lay on the bed and watch TV to get my mind off his behavior. He had disappeared into another room, and I wasn't about to go searching for him. I had drifted off to sleep when he climbed in bed and put his arms around me.

"Milton. Sweetheart, are you feeling better?" I inquired.

"I feel ok, baby." He responded.

"Then explain to me why you've been crying so much."

"Because I have put you through so much when the only thing you have done is love me."

"Milton, you have not hurt me, and I really wish you would stop saying that. You have brought unspeakable joy to my life, and unless I have missed something, you have not done anything wrong."

"Yes, I have. I haven't been very truthful with you."

"How so?" I questioned.

"Well, something from my past has come back to haunt me. Something that I haven't given any thought to in over three years."

I sat up in the bed and looked directly into his eyes. I couldn't wait to hear what he had to say. Then, it dawned on me that what he was speaking about was something that happened in the past, and I really didn't want to know about it.

"Milton, I personally feel that things that happened prior to you meeting me doesn't need to be discussed. I mean I have secrets that I've never told anyone from my past."

"Yeah, but your secret is not as devastating as mine could be." He said as he looked away.

"Since you feel that way, the only thing you can do is to tell me. But do you think it's really necessary for me to know?" I asked with a puzzled look on my face.

"Yes you definitely need to know. I'm not sure if you are going to want to be with me after I tell you."

He had my undivided attention at that point. I braced myself for more bad news. What could it possibly be? A child out of wedlock? A marriage?

"Ok, Milton. I'm listening." I said as my heart began pounding like bass drums.

"First, I just want you to know that I love you. Your happiness has been the most important thing to me…"

"Yeah, yeah, yeah! Will you just tell me!" I interrupted.

"Dae'Mon, I'm HIV positive. I'm so sorry!" Milton stated.

I didn't hear anything else he said after that. I thought that he might have been playing a joke on me, like one of those "Candid Camera" tricks. I could tell by the look on his face though that he was serious, and this was no laughing matter.

I tried to maintain my cool considering all Milton had just gone through, but I was losing control fast. A major bombshell had just been dropped on my doorstep without warning.

"Milton, you mean to tell me that you intentionally slept with me without disclosing your condition?"

"Baby, it wasn't like that." He responded.

"Don't baby me! You deceived me, Milton. You not once told me about your status. Not once! Milton, please go and leave me alone!"

"Dae'Mon, please try to understand." Milton pleaded.

"Understand! Understand! Milton! Are you stupid? Did you understand my damn feelings when you were fucking me without a rubber? Did you understand my feelings all those nights you said you love me? Did you once consider how I would feel? Did you?" I screamed. "Just get away from me."

"Dae'Mon, I'm so sorry."

"Sorry! That's best you can do is say you're sorry. Yeah, you are one sorry ass muthafucker. I hate you! I hate you, Milton Parker!" I screamed as tears flowed down my face like a raging river.

Milton grabbed me trying to comfort me, but I fought to get away from him. He was too strong. He rolled on top of me and held me in a tight embrace. The tears were endless. I felt my life disappearing before my eyes.

"Baby, let it out. We can get through this together." He said trying to comfort me.

"Milton, I thought you loved me? How could you destroy me like this? What did I ever do to you to deserve this? Why Milton? Why?" I cried out.

"Dae'Mon, I love you like I have never loved anyone before. I wish I could take it back, but I can't. Please believe me when I say I love you."

"Love don't live here anymore. Milton, I would have never done anything like this to you. Please let me go! I can't be around you anymore." I said as I struggled to free myself from his grasp.

Milton began to cry. "Dae'Mon, you said that you wouldn't leave me. You said that we could work through this together." He said as he held me tighter.

"That's before I found out that you ruined my life. You fucking bastard! You are going to burn in hell for what you've done to me. Just to think all this time I thought you were a man, but you ain't nothing but a bitch. A fucking

worthless bitch! I hate you! Let me go! Please! Let me go!"
I pleaded and screamed.

"Dae'Mon, you don't mean that. Baby, please let's talk
rationally." Milton said as he continued to hold on to me.

"I'm done talking to you. I just need to be alone right
now. I have to clear my head because I'm not thinking
straight." I said calmly.

I was trying reverse psychology to see if Milton would
buy it. He was smarter than I thought.

"Dae'Mon, I'm afraid that you're gonna leave if I let
you go. I need you! Please don't leave me Dae'Mon!
Please! I'll do anything in the world for you." Milton
begged.

"Don't beg. It doesn't become you. Besides, you've
done more than enough for me." I said sarcastically.
"Milton, yes I'm mad, but I promise you that I just want to
be alone right now to sort out my feelings. I'm not going
anywhere. I promise." I said.

Milton knew I was lying. I was talking and plotting my
escape at the same time. Part of me died the moment he told
me he was positive. There was no doubt in my mind that I
had been infected. Milton and I had unprotected sex too
many times for me not to have been.

I was angry with the fact that he didn't feel he could tell
me in the beginning. I'm not sure how I would have
responded, but I should have made the choice instead of
him making it for me.

"Ok Dae'Mon. If I let you go, will you promise me that
you're not going to leave and that we will talk about this
situation?" Milton questioned.

"Yes, I promise. I'm going into the other room to clear
my head, and we can talk in the morning."

Milton rolled off me. I jumped up from the bed and put
on my house shoes. He laid there with sadness in his eyes.
For a moment, I felt empathy for him. But when I thought
about what he did, I became enraged all over again.

"Dae'Mon, I know you're very angry with me, and you have every right to be. But I beg of you not to leave me. I don't know what I would do without you."

"Well Milton. If I leave, you have only yourself to blame." I said as I walked through the bedroom door into the hall.

I was surprised that Milton did not come after me. I discovered the reason why. I left the keys to my car on the nightstand, so he thought I wasn't going anywhere. That was his mistake. I had a spare key in my briefcase, which I kept in the downstairs office we shared.

I tiptoed downstairs to the office to retrieve my car key and cell phone. I heard Milton coming down the stairs, so I hid underneath the desk. When the coast was clear, I crawled to the kitchen and exited through the backdoor. Milton came running after me, but he was too slow. The elevator door closed before he could reach me.

I was confused and didn't know who to call. Justice had a man. Kevyn and I weren't speaking. Then, it hit me-Jamal. I hit the speed dial button for Jamal. He picked up on the first ring.

"Hello." Jamal said.

"Hey Jamal. This is Dae'Mon."

"Hey Dae'Mon, how are you?" He questioned.

"I'm not doing good. Can I come over?"

"Yes, sure you can. I'll be waiting for you."

"Ok, I'll see you in a bit." I said as I hung up the phone.

I was thankful that Jamal didn't live too far from the condo. I got in the car and cried all the way to his apartment. When he opened the door, I fell into his arms in tears. He just held me and didn't say a word.

CHAPTER THIRTY - FOUR

The water from my eyes continued to flow. I was in great pain and wasn't sure if I was going to survive. I stopped eating and no longer had a desire to live. I sunk deeper and deeper into depression. I would just cry myself to sleep only to wake up in tears.

Jamal had become a great comfort and support system for me. I had setup refuge at his place since the night I ran out on Milton. Jamal would hold me and caress me whenever I would cry. He never asked me what I was going through. Deep down inside, I think he knew. I felt guilty for leaning on him and not telling him what was going on in my life.

Milton had left several messages on my voice mail, but I refused to return any of his calls. He was in just as much pain as I was, but I couldn't find it in my heart to go to him. I wanted to hate him, but my heart wouldn't' allow me to do it. I still longed for his love. I was becoming more and more confused by the day. I didn't quite understand how I could still love him after what he had done to me.

My doctor advised me to take an HIV test, and I consented. He also suggested that I seek counseling once my results came back. I knew what the results were going to be. I didn't need a test to tell me that I was now a person living with the human immunodeficiency virus. How would I explain this to my family? I knew Big Mama would be devastated.

I agonized the two weeks it took for my test results to come back from the lab. I cried on a daily basis. No one should have to go through that wait. They should invent a way of telling you the same day to make the revelation less severe. Too much to ask for! I knew the test results would only confirm my worse fear, and just as I expected, my results indeed came back positive.

I sat in my doctor's office with a stone face. Expressionless! He was talking, but I wasn't hearing a word he was saying. I was thinking about how my life was over. How I wanted to fold up and die that very moment. I don't remember the outcome of the meeting. I just remember walking out of his office with the name and number of a therapist in hand.

I sobbed uncontrollably on the way back to Jamal's apartment. I had an idea, so I decided to return to the condo in hopes Milton would be there so I could kill him. My tears turned into pure rage. I could only see red, and I wasn't going to be satisfied until I squeezed the life out of his body.

He wasn't home, so I decided that I would call him at work to entice him to come home so I could carry out my murderous plot. Then, I would take my own life because it wasn't worth living anymore. I dialed Milton's cell phone.

"Hello, this is Milton." He said.

"Milton, this is Dae'Mon."

"Baby, I'm so glad you called. I've been worried about you. Are you all right? I've been calling everywhere trying to find you, but no one had seen or heard from you."

"I'm doing as well as a person can when they are living with a disease that's going to kill them. Are you happy now Milton? Are you happy that you have destroyed me?" I screamed into the phone.

"Baby, of course I'm not happy. I'm sorry for what I've put you through. You shouldn't have to go through this alone. Where are you? Are you home? I'm on my way. Baby, I'm so sorry and I love you so much. Please don't leave! Stay there until I get home! Please!" Milton pleaded.

"Yes I'll be here packing. I can't stand to be here anymore." I said as I slammed down the phone.

The river started to flow again. I crouched to the floor with my head between my knees and sobbed. Milton rushed into the bedroom to find me on the floor. He swooped me up in his arms and held me tightly. I cried out in pain as he held me. I didn't want to let go, but I knew I had to leave to find my way. Milton wiped my tears as water rolled down his face.

His face looked as if it had aged 20 years. No longer was that youthful look that I had grown accustomed to seeing. His eyes were puffy and blood shot red from lack of sleep. He told me that he hadn't slept since the night I left.

"Dae'Mon, I'm so happy that you're home. I was worried sick about you. Baby, I'm so sorry. I'm so sorry for what I've put you through!" he said as he cried.

"Milton, you keep saying that you're sorry, but you have yet to tell me why you did this?"

I raised up to a sitting position to face him. I wanted to look into his eyes to see if he was being deceitful.

"I got caught up in the moment and didn't think I would fall in love with you, but I did. I saw the joy and happiness in your eyes the night we first kissed, and I didn't think about it."

"Milton, that doesn't make sense. You met me for the first time three years ago, and you've known about your status for just as long. That's a cop out, saying that you just got caught up in the moment." I said as I stood up and began to pace back and forth.

"Dae'Mon, I didn't think that' I was, so that's why I never mentioned it to you. The only thing I wanted was you. You were the only person in this city who I thought would love me the way I wanted to be loved. I fell in love with you the moment I first laid eyes on you. You were the picture of love, and I knew someday, somehow I would be with you."

I stopped in mid-stride and turned to face Milton. My eyes were like piercing swords penetrating his skin.

"That's a very beautiful speech Milton. I'm so fucking happy for you! You certainly have a funny way of showing your love. You have done nothing more than lie and deceive me. Dae'Mon I want to love you like you've never been loved before. I'm going to give you the world. I promise you'll never have another worry. Now, look what you have done. And for the record, your type of love Mr. Parker I don't need. You are selfish and only out for yourself. You never cared about me because if you did I wouldn't' be in this predicament. You have ruined my life once, but I will not give you the opportunity to do it again. As the saying goes, fuck me once shame on you, fuck me twice shame on me."

Milton reached out for me as I headed to the closet. I hurried my steps so that he couldn't touch me.

"Milton, keep your fucking hands off of me. I'm leaving, and there's nothing you can do to stop me."

"Dae'Mon, please don't leave me! I beg of you to stay so we can work through this together." Milton cried.

"It's a little too late for us to be working together. You should have thought about working together when we first met. Now, you can work with yo fucking self!" I yelled as I began to pull my suitcases out of the closets.

"Dae'Mon, what can I do to get you to stay? Do I have to get down on my hands and knees and beg?" Milton questioned.

"Yeah, why don't you get down on all fours and crawl like the dog that you are. There's nothing you can do for me other than get the fuck up out of my face. Go back to work! You're dismissed. Being the compassionate person that I am, I will leave you the address and phone number to where I will be staying. I only want you to send my mail to me and don't call unless you have died."

"Dae'Mon, you're being cruel." Milton said.

"Oh, now that's a very interesting statement. I'm the cruel one. But you're a saint. Let me tell you something, you were the one who screwed our relationship up by not telling me about your HIV status. You were the one who intentionally lied to me, so that makes you the cruel one, asshole. Milton, please leave me alone! I have to finish packing so I can get out of your sight for good."

"Dae'Mon, I can't make it without you. I just might kill myself." Milton responded.

"Do you need any help? I won't shed one tear if you do because you have already killed me."

I finished packing the clothes that I was going to take with me and headed to the bathroom to retrieve my vanity items. Milton followed me into the bathroom with a depressive look on his face. As mad as I was with him, it still tore me up inside to see him this way. I just wasn't sure if I could love him anymore.

I finished packing and was about to leave. But I decided I had to do one more thing before I left. I walked over to Milton and pulled him up to me. I planted a deep passionate kiss on his juicy lips. I pulled back.

"Just so you'll know what you'll be missing and will never get again." I said as I turned to walk away.

"Dae'Mon, please don't do this! I beg of you." Milton said as he began to sob.

I grabbed my luggage and headed for the door. Milton followed me with tear-stained eyes and fell in the middle of the living room floor sobbing uncontrollably. I closed the door behind me. Tears welled up in my eyes, but I refused to let them flow.

I walked away from the one man I truly loved and the place I called home. I was headed out into the sunset not sure where I was going to end up. But one thing I knew for sure, my life had changed forever.

CHAPTER THIRTY - FIVE

My Dearest Dae'Mon,

I can only imagine the pain and agony that you're going through right now. I'm sure words cannot describe your feelings. It hurts me deeply to know that I'm responsible. I apologize from the bottom of my heart.

I'm sure that you're confused about everything that has transpired over the past few weeks. I will do my best to shed light on the situation, so you will be able to put all the pieces of the puzzle together.

It was during my stay in the hospital after the car accident that my past came back to haunt me. When I was first diagnosed in 1996, I thought the doctors had made a mistake since I was so healthy and in good shape. In essence, I blocked the thought from my mind and had not thought of my status in years. Then, Dr. Wright asked me if I would consent to having a routine blood check. I didn't think anything of it, so I gave my permission. That's when it was discovered that my blood contained the HIV virus. I had to finally accept the fact that I was indeed positive.

I knew I had to find a way to tell you without making you feel that you had been deceived. I knew it wasn't going to be easy disclosing my condition to you, but it was imperative that I did. Upon seeing your beautiful face as you walked into the hospital room, I couldn't help but to cry. I knew I had put your life in jeopardy, and it saddened me. I was also very afraid of losing your love. I wanted to go back in time to erase history, but I knew I couldn't.

Your love had become the most important thing to me. As selfish as this may sound, I just didn't think I could live without you. So, I kept my secret hidden. Every time a situation arouse where I wanted to disclose my status to you, my mouth paralyzed me. I just couldn't force myself to say the words. Now, that paralysis has cost me the love of my life.

I was crazy about you from the moment I first laid eyes on you; and when I kissed you for the first time, I knew you were the one for me. I fell in love with you almost immediately, which was something that I didn't think would happen especially after the relationship I had a few years prior to meeting you. I was left feeling bitter and withdrawn and didn't think I would ever recover. Then, I laid eyes on the most beautiful man in the world when you strolled by me that night at Connections.

I know I have hurt you a great deal. I just hope that one day you will be able to find it in your heart to forgive me.

My days and nights are lonely without you. I find myself reaching for you sometimes late at night only to find that you're not beside me. I have cried myself to sleep more nights than I care to remember. I just wish I could hold you again.

I have accepted the fact that you may never want to see me again, but I hope that's not the case. I'm hoping that you will someday come to love me again.

I will await your response. I hope to hear from you soon.

With All My Love,

Milton

P.S. I will never stop loving you.

THE END FOR NOW

About The Author

A 1994 graduate of the University of Kansas with a degree in theatre and film, J. Aundre' Clinton makes his literary debut with Sins From the Past. Mr. Clinton is an active tennis player and avid sports fan. Rock Chalk Jayhawk. KU! He resides in Atlanta, Georgia where he is at work on his second novel.